THE ROAD
AND OTH

T0082289

One hundred years after its
"The Road Not Taken" remains among our best-loved
poems, and its author perhaps our most widely read poet.
The poem's premise, drawn from Frost's walks and conver-
sations with the poet Edward Thomas, appears simple: a
man at a fork in the road, either physical or metaphorical,
chooses a path to follow. Yet line by line, we are tangled in
contradictions and complexities. "The Road Not Taken" is
a story about the stories we tell about ourselves and our
world—stories full of doubt and possibility that, taken
together, determine how we view the life we are leading,
and how we will think about the life we have led. For Frost,
poetry was, as he once put it, "the one permissible way of
saying one thing and meaning another." Nowhere is that
more evident than in this classic lyric and its fellow early
poems, whose resistance to resolution has kept them enchant-
ing and challenging after a century of reading.

The Road Not Taken and Other Poems celebrates the
100th anniversary of "The Road Not Taken," published in
the August 1915 issue of the *Atlantic Monthly*. This volume
presents Frost's essential early poems, selected by award-
winning poetry critic David Orr.

"He has bequeathed his nation a body of imperishable verse
from which Americans will forever gain joy and under-
standing."   —JOHN F. KENNEDY

"By the time he was forty and had finished his second book,
North of Boston, he had arrived. Step by step, he had tested
his observation of places and people until his best poems
had the human and seen richness of great novels. No one
had helped him to learn, and now no one could because no
one wrote better."   —ROBERT LOWELL

PENGUIN CLASSICS (🐧) DELUXE EDITION

THE ROAD NOT TAKEN
AND OTHER POEMS

ROBERT FROST was born in San Francisco in 1874 and moved to Lawrence, Massachusetts, as a young boy. After briefly attending Dartmouth and Harvard, he worked as a teacher and chicken farmer while writing poetry at night. In 1912, Frost moved to England with his family, where he befriended poets like Ezra Pound, F. S. Flint, and, most importantly, Edward Thomas. He returned to America in 1915, where the publication of his first two books, *A Boy's Will* and *North of Boston*, established him as one of the most essential poets of his time. Over the next five decades, Frost published nine more volumes of poetry, earning four Pulitzer Prizes and a Congressional Gold Medal. He died in Boston in 1963, leaving a body of work that remains among the greatest in American poetry.

DAVID ORR is the poetry columnist for the *New York Times Book Review*, and he teaches at Cornell University. He is the winner of the Nona Balakian Citation for Excellence in Reviewing from the National Book Critics Circle and the Editor's Prize for Reviewing from *Poetry* magazine. He holds a BA from Princeton and a JD from Yale Law School.

ROBERT FROST

The Road Not Taken and Other Poems

100<small>TH</small>-ANNIVERSARY EDITION

Edited with an Introduction by
DAVID ORR

PENGUIN BOOKS

PENGUIN BOOKS

An imprint of Penguin Random House LLC
375 Hudson Street
New York, New York 10014
penguin.com

This edition published in Penguin Books 2015

LIBRARY OF CONGRESS CATALOGING-IN-PUBLICATION DATA
Frost, Robert, 1874–1963.
[Poems. Selections]
The Road Not Taken and other poems / Robert Frost ; edited and with an introduction by
David Orr.—100th-Anniversary edition.
pages cm.—(Penguin Classics deluxe)
ISBN 978-0-14-310739-2 (paperback)
I. Orr, David, 1974– editor. II. Title.
PS3511.R94A6 2015
811'.52—dc23   2015023806

Printed in the United States of America
14th Printing

Set in Sabon LT Std
Designed by Sabrina Bowers

Contents

THE ROAD NOT TAKEN
AND OTHER POEMS

Introduction

In the later stages of his strange, illustrious, and very long career, Robert Frost was often talked about as if he were two different poets, or possibly even two different people— a phenomenon that continues even now, half a century after his death in 1963. The first poet is the familiar New England icon, the salty, no-nonsense dispenser of rustic wisdom whose lines have the sturdiness and warmth of hearthstones knelt upon by generations of yeoman farmers. This Frost is the Robert Frost of the common reader, the Frost of birches and fields and snow and spring pools. He writes plain poems that make plain sense, or seem to. Those poems often rhyme, and when they do, they do so forthrightly (*deep* and *sleep*, for instance). They're frequently about the quotidian lives of farmers, day laborers, mill workers, and other small-time folk at the beginning of the twentieth century. Their stanzas slat tidily together, like the corners of log cabins, and their most memorable lines are the sort of homely epigrams you might find crocheted on throw pillows: "I took the one less traveled by"; "Good fences make good neighbours"; "But all the fun's in how you say a thing." This Robert Frost feels a bit old-fashioned, maybe, but in the way that George Washington seems old-fashioned, or pilgrim hats on Thanksgiving. He's part of the bedrock of the American identity.

The second Frost—"the other Frost," as Randall Jarrell described him in 1953—is nearly the opposite of the first. This Frost is dark, manipulative, and withholding. His poems are often about madness or violence, and their seemingly stable surfaces are sheets of ice through which the unwitting traveler can easily plunge into frigid water. This Frost was no provincial farmer-poet, but rather a ruthlessly competitive and immensely erudite artist who was far more widely traveled than peers often considered more cosmopolitan, like Wallace Stevens. This Frost is the Frost of the sophisticated reader and, more specifically, the academic reader. Understanding this Robert Frost usually entails rejecting the first Frost as a pretense ("the great act," as Robert Lowell once labeled it). It often means rejecting the audience who believes in that act as well. As the critic Lionel Trilling put it in a birthday salute to Frost in 1959, "I have undertaken to say that a great many of your admirers have not understood clearly what you have been doing in your life in poetry." If the first Frost resembles one of the great carved heads of Mount Rushmore—half monument, half kitsch, and accessible to anyone willing to pay for parking— the second Frost often seems more like the surrounding badlands, where only a fool travels without a guide. And between these two possibilities is an obscuring, dust-filled haze.

It's tempting to say that the truth must lie hidden somewhere in the middle of that uncertain divide. If Frost isn't really a gruff but good-natured national bard, then surely it's equally wrong to try to turn him into a cold-eyed aesthete. The actual poet must be some blend of the two. But rather than wondering who or what Robert Frost really was, it's more interesting to wonder why his identity seems to matter in the first place. Few readers, for example, worry over whether Ezra Pound was "really" something entirely different from the Ezra Pound one reads about in the introduction to, say, *Early Writings* (Penguin Classics, 2005). The same goes for T. S. Eliot, Marianne Moore, William Carlos Williams—all of Frost's renowned peers. Why do we care where the essence of Frost truly resides, and whom that essence was truly for?

The answer to this question is complex. But one aspect of it is simple: Frost became a public figure in a way no other American poet has managed, or even come close to managing. His goodwill was courted not just by scholars and other writers but by presidents and senators. He routinely spent the night at Eisenhower's White House; he was good friends with Stewart Udall, John F. Kennedy's secretary of the interior; and he was sent to the Soviet Union by Kennedy himself, where he spoke at length and privately with Nikita Khrushchev. (To appreciate how extraordinary this was, try to imagine a contemporary American poet being directed to Russia by President Obama and securing a tête-à-tête with Vladimir Putin.) Readers bought his works in numbers that would today be respectable for a fairly popular novelist, but that for a poet in the first half of the twentieth century were well beyond staggering. By the time his *Complete Poems* was issued in 1949, more than four hundred thousand of his books had been sold. That same year, a copy of Frost's first, privately printed collection was auctioned for the equivalent of thirty thousand dollars in today's currency, "a price thought to be the highest paid for a work by a contemporary American author," according to the *New York Times*. When he died, his obituary ran on the front page of the *Times*, and included this tribute from

Kennedy: "I think politicians and poets share at least one thing, and that is their greatness depends upon the courage with which they face the challenges of life." Since Frost's death, his legacy has practically become a national resource, and like any resource, it tempts people to seize pieces of it for themselves. Given that, it's probably not surprising that there have come to be multiple versions of Frost. When we want to lay claim to something, we put forward the image that seems most favorable for our possession.

Of course, at the beginning there were no images at all, only the very young Robert Frost—Robert *Lee* Frost, actually, for the Confederate general. That middle name may seem odd for a poet who would come to be so closely identified with New England, but in fact, most of Frost's early life had very little to do with the Yankee farming milieu he later embodied. He was born in San Francisco in 1874, the son of a firebrand newspaperman (and Robert E. Lee admirer) and a shy Swedenborgian schoolteacher. Frost didn't set foot on the soil of New England until he was eleven years old, when the death of his father forced his mother to turn to the support of her in-laws in Massachusetts. The family eventually settled in Salem Depot, New Hampshire, where Frost quickly distinguished himself as an excellent student, particularly in the classics, and a hard-charging athlete.

Frost's formative years were dominated by two overriding and entwined passions. The first, as one might expect, was for poetry, which he appears to have begun writing around age sixteen (his earliest known poem is about a Spanish retreat during the conquest of Mexico). The second was for Elinor White, with whom he shared valedictory honors in his high school class. Their courtship was turbulent. Frost wanted to be married right away, but Elinor put him off; she wanted to finish college, and she also wanted Frost to secure some means of support. Frost's own relationship with higher education was ambivalent at best, despite his intense interest in philosophy and literature. He entered Dartmouth in the fall of 1892, but he dropped out after less than a year, lonely and impatient with the regimented nature of university instruction, and returned to courting Elinor. When his first published poem, "My Butterfly," was accepted by one of New York's weekly magazines, he took this as an occasion to press his suit. He had a small book of five poems printed up and traveled to Elinor's college in order to deliver it by hand. When this failed to bring about the anticipated swoon, Frost fled to a swamp on the Virginia–North Carolina border, where he wandered around in a fit of extravagant despair until rescued by a group of duck hunters. Upon returning, he devoted himself again to Elinor, this time a bit more calmly, and they were finally married in December of 1895. Frost was twenty-one.

The next fifteen years would include a series of moves across New England, the death of Frost's mother, the loss of two of the couple's six children (their first child died from cholera; their sixth lived only three days), and a parade of temporary jobs for Frost: reporter, teacher, tutor, chicken farmer of questionable distinction. (Much of Frost's writing from this period appeared in magazines like *The Eastern Poultryman* and *Farm-Poultry*.) Through all of it, Frost wrote poetry with relentless focus, even though his efforts were routinely rejected by leading editors in New York and Boston. Left with little to go on but his own nerve, he developed a sense of self-reliance that was as unrepentant as it was unforgiving. In "Into My

Own," the first poem in his first book, he writes of setting out alone into a limitless, primeval forest:

> I do not see why I should e'er turn back,
> Or those should not set forth upon my track
> To overtake me, who should miss me here
> And long to know if still I held them dear.
>
> They would not find me changed from him they knew—
> Only more sure of all I thought was true.

One sees here the vestiges of Victorianism (*e'er*) that Frost would soon discard, as well as the confident, conversational meter that would eventually make his poems unmistakable, and in many cases unforgettable. Despite his setbacks, he was sure of the worth of his writing. In 1912, with the assistance of a legacy from Frost's grandfather (whose support he had grudgingly relied on for years), he and Elinor decided to move to England in a last-ditch attempt to ignite the literary career that had thus far thrown off only a few quickly extinguished sparks.

The move was a spectacular success. Frost quickly met many of the leading poets circling London—among them F. S. Flint and the ubiquitous Ezra Pound—and within a year, he had placed his first book with a British publisher. But the most important contact that Frost made in his time in England was with the journalist (and later poet) Edward Thomas. Thomas almost immediately recognized the significance of Frost's poetry, and his early reviews were essential in establishing the terms by which Frost would be discussed on both sides of the Atlantic. He remains one of Frost's finest critics. Here is what he said about Frost in July of 1914:

This is one of the most revolutionary books of modern times, but one of the quietest and least aggressive. . . . These poems are revolutionary because they lack the exaggeration of rhetoric, and even at first sight appear to lack the poetic intensity of which rhetoric is an imitation. Their language is free from the poetical words and forms that are the chief material of secondary poets. The metre avoids not only the old-fashioned pomp and sweetness, but the later fashion also of discord and fuss. In fact, the medium is common speech.

As Thomas understood, there is a kind of easy natural-ness to Frost's writing that mimics ordinary talk, and that achieves a similarly vast range of effects and tones. The two writers soon became close friends, with Thomas pro-viding Frost the responsive, companionable intelligence he'd longed for, and Frost giving Thomas the encourage-ment to write his own (very good) poetry.

Frost and his family returned from England in 1915, just ahead of German U-boats. Recognition in England had landed Frost an American publisher, and upon arriving in New York, he was greeted with a glowing review of his second book, *North of Boston*, by Amy Lowell in *The New Republic*. (Frost's first two books were published in reverse order in the United States, with *North of Boston* appear-ing two months before *A Boy's Will*.) If Frost's early years were lonely and unrewarding, at least in professional terms, his literary life after his return to America was practically charmed: within two years, he had accepted a lucrative po-sition at Amherst (one of many university appointments he would eventually hold); within nine years, he had won the Pulitzer Prize, the first of four he would be awarded.

He was hugely in demand as a lecturer and reader, and began to develop the persona that would become his trademark. Jay Parini, Frost's most judicious biographer, describes that role as "the slow-talking, witty, wisecracking, rueful, commonsensical, quasi-philosophical man of letters—a carefully composed mask no less artful than those constructed by Oscar Wilde or Mark Twain before him." He seemed half sage, half farmer, and audiences loved him.

Politicians loved him too. As I said, no American poet before or since has occupied such a prominent place in the political life of the United States. Frost's private existence became increasingly dark over the years—Elinor died, his son Carol committed suicide, and his daughter Irma became increasingly unstable (he eventually committed her to an asylum). But his public life was lived in unremitting sunlight. When he turned seventy-five, the Senate passed a resolution congratulating him for "setting forth to our minds a reliable representation of ourselves and all men"; when he turned eighty-five, the same body gave him a gold medal. Shortly after his death in 1963 at age eighty-eight, President Kennedy spoke at the dedication of the Robert Frost Library at Amherst. He called the poet "one of the granite figures of our time," adding, "He was supremely two things: an artist and an American."

If this biographical sketch seems to have passed rather quickly over the years in which Frost became famous enough to be asked for autographs, that's no accident. It is Frost's strongest poetry, not his biography, that makes him worth reading today, and that poetry was written largely in his youth and early middle age. Frost would produce a few notable poems later in life—most significantly

"Directive," which first appeared in 1946—but the Frost we think of today is almost completely the product of work produced well before World War II, in the two decades bracketing his sojourn in England.

And it is this early writing, not his eventual celebrity, that most strongly encourages readers to set themselves in camps dedicated to opposing images of the poet. The defining feature of Frost's poetry is its resistance to definitions, a near paradox that Frost would have enjoyed. He thought of poems less as static objects than as bodies in constant, athletic motion; as soon as you feel you've gotten a glimpse of one aspect of the poem (and the poet), the lines pivot and the vision changes. To appreciate the singularity of this effect within the context of Frost's time, it's helpful to look at two influential remarks about poetry, the first by Frost's great peer and rival, T. S. Eliot, and the second by Frost himself. Here is Eliot writing about *Hamlet* in 1921:

> The only way of expressing emotion in the form of art is by finding an "objective correlative"; in other words, a set of objects, a situation, a chain of events which shall be the formula of that *particular* emotion; such that when the external facts, which must terminate in sensory experience, are given, the emotion is immediately evoked.

And here is Frost writing to his friend Louis Untermeyer in 1917:

> You get more credit for thinking if you restate formulae or cite cases that fall in easily under formulae, but all the fun is outside saying things that suggest formulae that won't formulate—that almost but don't quite formulate. I should

like to be so subtle at this game as to seem to the casual person altogether obvious.

Eliot believed the experience of the reader should reflect the emotional intention of the poet as by formula—by an "objective correlative"—even if the connection might be obscure. Thus we have *The Waste Land*, with its scattered cultural rubble as a stand-in for the poet's own internal turmoil: "These fragments I have shored against my ruins." Eliot might be difficult, but he is *straightforwardly* difficult. Frost, on the other hand, wanted to "suggest formulae that won't formulate—that almost but don't quite formulate." Against a background of what he once called "black and utter chaos," he refused to defend a fixed position, relying instead on a performer's shape-shifting agility to avoid entanglements he couldn't slip loose of, including overly earnest entanglements with the reader. The relationship he sought was premised instead on teasing, flirting, gamesmanship. "Poetry," as he once said, "provides the one permissible way of saying one thing and meaning another."

Of course, to place this much emphasis on the disconnection between what we say (or write) and what we actually mean is to come very close to being deceptive. Frost was well aware of that; he didn't mind seeming "altogether obvious" even if the obviousness was a pose. The pose, in a sense, was the point: the very mechanism that makes Frost's poems so successful also makes them work their way between audiences like tiny splinters, separating us into the saved (who understand), the damned (who don't), the damned who think they're saved, and so on in an endless cycle of interpretation.

To see how this works in practice, we could turn to

nearly any of the poems gathered here. Most of these demonstrate one or more of Frost's favorite tactics for avoiding anything "formulaic," the most obvious of which is what you might call intentional abuse of a stock formula—or just plain old clumsiness on purpose. Frost is the only major American poet who is perfectly willing to let readers think he's done something a Hallmark card writer might balk at. This is often a matter of deliberately thumping, predictable rhyming, as in "Bond and Free," which concludes by pairing *star* with *far* (though he had a superb ear, Frost almost never used slant rhyme, a technique that would have allowed him to show off his acuity, as Yeats does in "Sailing to Byzantium" by rhyming *wall*, *soul*, and *animal*). But more subtly and pervasively, we see Frost's cultivated clumsiness in the sheer plainness of long passages in even his best poems. In "The Black Cottage," for example, Frost gives us a man out on a walk with his minister. They come across the cottage of an old woman from the minister's congregation who has died relatively recently, and the minister begins a very long description of the house and its occupant that is notably lacking in the fire and brimstone of poetry:

> A buttoned hair-cloth lounge spread scrolling arms
> Under a crayon portrait on the wall
> Done sadly from an old daguerreotype.
> That was the father as he went to war.
> She always, when she talked about war,
> Sooner or later came and leaned, half knelt
> Against the lounge beside it, though I doubt
> If such unlifelike lines kept power to stir
> Anything in her after all the years.
> He fell at Gettysburg or Fredricksburg,

> I ought to know—it makes a difference which:
> Fredricksburg wasn't Gettysburg, of course.
> But what I'm getting to is how forsaken
> A little cottage this has always seemed . . .

"But what I'm getting to": this is the kind of expression that seems dull in conversation, let alone a poem. In one of the best commentaries on "The Black Cottage," the critic William Pritchard acknowledges that the relatively slack passage above can come across as "simply not very interesting." But as Pritchard goes on to observe, that slackness provides a necessary contrast for the very different register the poem reaches in its conclusion. As the minister thinks about the nature of the ideas to which the old widow was devoted, and the way our beliefs often seem untethered to any factual support, his speech strengthens and blooms. He imagines a land dedicated to truths that have gone out of fashion:

> I wish
> I could be monarch of a desert land
> I could devote and dedicate forever
> To the truths we keep coming back and back to.
> So desert it would have to be, so walled
> By mountain ranges half in summer snow,
> No one would covet it or think it worth
> The pains of conquering to force change on.
> Scattered oases where men dwelt, but mostly
> Sand dunes held loosely in tamarisk
> Blown over and over themselves in idleness.
> Sand grains should sugar in the natal dew
> The babe born to the desert, the sand storm
> Retard mid-waste my cowering caravans . . .

"Sand grains should sugar in the natal dew": the sudden, surprising richness of the language is like the flourish of a magician's cape. We thought we saw only a battered felt hat, but now suddenly, everywhere there are birds, birds, birds.

And Frost, like a magician, is a master of the prolonged moment, of the deliberate introduction of seemingly unimportant or unrelated information just when we're expecting a poem to crystallize around an image or message. In "The Mountain," for instance, a traveler in the shadow of a mountain encounters an old man driving a cart. Conversation ensues, and we think the poem is about to focus on a spring on the mountain's summit, which the old man describes as being miraculously "cold in summer, warm in winter." But then the old man starts talking about views from the top (which he's never seen), then the opinion of a man who may have gone to the top ("'He said there was a lake / Somewhere in Ireland on a mountain top.' // 'But a lake's different. What about the spring?'"). Then we get an amusingly banal diversion into the name of the mountain ("'We call it Hor: I don't know if that's right.'"). When Frost finally returns us to the spring at the end of the poem, we discover that the spring is simply water at a constant temperature:

"I don't suppose the water's changed at all.
You and I know enough to know it's warm
Compared with cold, and cold compared with warm.
But all the fun's in how you say a thing."

To the extent there's a point, then, that point is simply "fun": the way language blurs the arguments we thought might grow distinct, and unsettles the descriptions we thought might become stable.

Nowhere is this more evident than in "The Road Not Taken," the much-quoted, sepia-toned poem from which this volume takes its title. It reads in full:

Two roads diverged in a yellow wood,
And sorry I could not travel both
And be one traveler, long I stood
And looked down one as far as I could
To where it bent in the undergrowth;

Then took the other, as just as fair,
And having perhaps the better claim,
Because it was grassy and wanted wear;
Though as for that the passing there
Had worn them really about the same,

And both that morning equally lay
In leaves no step had trodden black.
Oh, I kept the first for another day!
Yet knowing how way leads on to way,
I doubted if I should ever come back.

I shall be telling this with a sigh
Somewhere ages and ages hence:
Two roads diverged in a wood, and I—
I took the one less traveled by,
And that has made all the difference.

You may have assumed, as most people do, that "The Road Not Taken" is a salute to rugged individualism. But this isn't the case: the poem's famous final lines, which assert that taking the road "less traveled by" has made "all the differ-ence," are flatly contradicted by the preceding stanzas, in which it becomes clear that the two roads are, in fact, practically identical ("the passing there / Had worn them really about the same, // And both that morning equally lay / In leaves . . ."). The poem is therefore more literally read as an illustration of the way that we like to deceive ourselves about the control we exercise over the direction of our lives. It's a parable about making stories up after the fact, not bravely venturing down challenging paths—indeed, it's almost a parody of its own most popular interpretation. This misunderstanding has become moderately famous, to the extent that every ten years or so, a journalist undertakes to explain what everyone has gotten wrong. (My favorite of these corrections occurs in a conversation among three prison inmates on the Netflix show *Orange Is the New Black*.)

And yet Frost doesn't fully commit to this "correct" reading either. Instead, he loads the poem with a jumble of ambiguous or confusing elements. Why is the road "less traveled" (or not) rather than simply "more difficult," as readers often suppose? What should we make of the apparent redundancy of declaring that you're sorry you can't "travel both / And be one traveler"? Why is the narrator sighing, and how should we take the tone of that sigh? (Frost used to tell audiences that the tone—whatever it was—was "absolutely saving.") Why say that the choice makes "all the difference"—which could be good or bad—instead of something less ambiguous, like "all the success"? In combination, these elements prevent "The Road Not Taken" from moving smoothly into a parody of self-affirmation. Frost keeps the lines from stabilizing, leaving the poem in a state of flux between the triumphant story of perseverance that it isn't and the wicked joke that it isn't quite. We can't be entirely sure what to make of it, or of its creator. We think we have it, we lose it, we gain it again in a meandering, teasing pursuit before an ever-retreating horizon—and if there were ever any one, "true" Frost, that perpetually dissolving boundary is where we would find him.

DAVID ORR

A Note on the Text

This Penguin Classics Deluxe Edition offers a selection of Robert Frost's most admired early poems as chosen by David Orr to commemorate the 100th anniversary of the publication of "The Road Not Taken." The poems herein generally follow the first printings of *A Boy's Will*, *North of Boston*, and *Mountain Interval*, although several typographical errors in those versions have been corrected in keeping with suggestions put forward by Tim Kendall in *The Art of Robert Frost* (Yale University Press). In addition, because this is a selected volume, the formatting has been regularized where it seemed appropriate for a book of this nature; for instance, "The Pasture" is not printed in italics, and the prose glosses have been removed from the table of contents entries taken from *A Boy's Will*. Readers interested in a full reproduction of Frost's early work should refer to *Early Poems* (Penguin Classics, 1998), which includes an introduction, suggestions for further reading, and notes by Robert Faggen.

The Road Not Taken
and Other Poems

FROM

A Boy's Will

(1913)

Into My Own

One of my wishes is that those dark trees,
So old and firm they scarcely show the breeze,
Were not, as 'twere, the merest mask of gloom,
But stretched away unto the edge of doom.

5 I should not be withheld but that some day
Into their vastness I should steal away,
Fearless of ever finding open land,
Or highway where the slow wheel pours the sand.

I do not see why I should e'er turn back,
10 Or those should not set forth upon my track
To overtake me, who should miss me here
And long to know if still I held them dear.

They would not find me changed from him they knew—
Only more sure of all I thought was true.

A Late Walk

When I go up through the mowing field,
   The headless aftermath,
Smooth-laid like thatch with the heavy dew,
   Half closes the garden path.

5 And when I come to the garden ground,
   The whir of sober birds
Up from the tangle of withered weeds
   Is sadder than any words.

A tree beside the wall stands bare,
10   But a leaf that lingered brown,
Disturbed, I doubt not, by my thought,
   Comes softly rattling down.

I end not far from my going forth
   By picking the faded blue
15 Of the last remaining aster flower
   To carry again to you.

Stars

How countlessly they congregate
   O'er our tumultuous snow,
Which flows in shapes as tall as trees
   When wintry winds do blow!—

5 As if with keenness for our fate,
   Our faltering few steps on
To white rest, and a place of rest
   Invisible at dawn,—

And yet with neither love nor hate,
10 Those stars like some snow-white
Minerva's snow-white marble eyes
   Without the gift of sight.

Storm Fear

When the wind works against us in the dark,
And pelts with snow
The lower chamber window on the east,
And whispers with a sort of stifled bark,
5   The beast,
"Come out! Come out!"—
It costs no inward struggle not to go,
Ah, no!
I count our strength,
10   Two and a child,
Those of us not asleep subdued to mark
How the cold creeps as the fire dies at length,—
How drifts are piled,
Dooryard and road ungraded,
15   Till even the comforting barn grows far away
And my heart owns a doubt
Whether 'tis in us to arise with day
And save ourselves unaided.

Wind and Window Flower

Lovers, forget your love,
   And list to the love of these,
She a window flower,
   And he a winter breeze.

5 When the frosty window veil
   Was melted down at noon,
And the caged yellow bird
   Hung over her in tune,

He marked her through the pane,
10   He could not help but mark,
And only passed her by,
   To come again at dark.

He was a winter wind,
   Concerned with ice and snow,
15 Dead weeds and unmated birds,
   And little of love could know.

But he sighed upon the sill,
   He gave the sash a shake,
As witness all within
20   Who lay that night awake.

Perchance he half prevailed
   To win her for the flight

From the firelit looking-glass
    And warm stove-window light.

25   But the flower leaned aside
        And thought of naught to say,
    And morning found the breeze
        A hundred miles away.

Flower-Gathering

I left you in the morning,
And in the morning glow,
You walked a way beside me
To make me sad to go.
5 Do you know me in the gloaming,
Gaunt and dusty grey with roaming?
Are you dumb because you know me not,
Or dumb because you know?

All for me? And not a question
10 For the faded flowers gay
That could take me from beside you
For the ages of a day?
They are yours, and be the measure
Of their worth for you to treasure,
15 The measure of the little while
That I've been long away.

In Neglect

They leave us so to the way we took,
    As two in whom they were proved mistaken,
That we sit sometimes in the wayside nook,
With mischievous, vagrant, seraphic look,
5   And *try* if we cannot feel forsaken.

Mowing

There was never a sound beside the wood but one,
And that was my long scythe whispering to the ground.
What was it it whispered? I knew not well myself;
Perhaps it was something about the heat of the sun,
5 Something, perhaps, about the lack of sound—
And that was why it whispered and did not speak.
It was no dream of the gift of idle hours,
Or easy gold at the hand of fay or elf:
Anything more than the truth would have seemed too weak
10 To the earnest love that laid the swale in rows,
Not without feeble-pointed spikes of flowers
(Pale orchises), and scared a bright green snake.
The fact is the sweetest dream that labor knows.
My long scythe whispered and left the hay to make.

Revelation

We make ourselves a place apart
    Behind light words that tease and flout,
But oh, the agitated heart
    Till someone find us really out.

5 'Tis pity if the case require
    (Or so we say) that in the end
We speak the literal to inspire
    The understanding of a friend.

But so with all, from babes that play
10   At hide-and-seek to God afar,
So all who hide too well away
    Must speak and tell us where they are.

The Trial by Existence

Even the bravest that are slain
    Shall not dissemble their surprise
On waking to find valor reign,
    Even as on earth, in paradise;
5 And where they sought without the sword
    Wide fields of asphodel fore'er,
To find that the utmost reward
    Of daring should be still to dare.

The light of heaven falls whole and white
10   And is not shattered into dyes,
The light for ever is morning light;
    The hills are verdured pasture-wise;
The angel hosts with freshness go,
    And seek with laughter what to brave;—
15 And binding all is the hushed snow
    Of the far-distant breaking wave.

And from a cliff-top is proclaimed
    The gathering of the souls for birth,
The trial by existence named,
20   The obscuration upon earth.
And the slant spirits trooping by
    In streams and cross- and counter-streams
Can but give ear to that sweet cry
    For its suggestion of what dreams!

25   And the more loitering are turned
         To view once more the sacrifice
     Of those who for some good discerned
         Will gladly give up paradise.
     And a white shimmering concourse rolls
30   Toward the throne to witness there
     The speeding of devoted souls
         Which God makes his especial care.

     And none are taken but who will,
         Having first heard the life read out
35   That opens earthward, good and ill,
         Beyond the shadow of a doubt;
     And very beautifully God limns,
         And tenderly, life's little dream,
     But naught extenuates or dims,
40   Setting the thing that is supreme.

     Nor is there wanting in the press
         Some spirit to stand simply forth,
     Heroic in its nakedness,
         Against the uttermost of earth.
45   The tale of earth's unhonored things
         Sounds nobler there than 'neath the sun;
     And the mind whirls and the heart sings,
         And a shout greets the daring one.

     But always God speaks at the end:
50   "One thought in agony of strife
     The bravest would have by for friend,
         The memory that he chose the life;
     But the pure fate to which you go
         Admits no memory of choice,

55 Or the woe were not earthly woe
    To which you give the assenting voice."

And so the choice must be again,
    But the last choice is still the same;
And the awe passes wonder then,
60   And a hush falls for all acclaim.
And God has taken a flower of gold
    And broken it, and used therefrom
The mystic link to bind and hold
    Spirit to matter till death come.

65 'Tis of the essence of life here,
    Though we choose greatly, still to lack
The lasting memory at all clear,
    That life has for us on the wrack
Nothing but what we somehow chose;
70   Thus are we wholly stripped of pride
In the pain that has but one close,
    Bearing it crushed and mystified.

The Tuft of Flowers

I went to turn the grass once after one
Who mowed it in the dew before the sun.

The dew was gone that made his blade so keen
Before I came to view the levelled scene.

5   I looked for him behind an isle of trees;
I listened for his whetstone on the breeze.

But he had gone his way, the grass all mown,
And I must be, as he had been,—alone,

"As all must be," I said within my heart,
10   "Whether they work together or apart."

But as I said it, swift there passed me by
On noiseless wing a 'wildered butterfly,

Seeking with memories grown dim o'er night
Some resting flower of yesterday's delight.

15   And once I marked his flight go round and round,
As where some flower lay withering on the ground.

And then he flew as far as eye could see,
And then on tremulous wing came back to me.

I thought of questions that have no reply,
20   And would have turned to toss the grass to dry;

But he turned first, and led my eye to look
At a tall tuft of flowers beside a brook,

A leaping tongue of bloom the scythe had spared
Beside a reedy brook the scythe had bared.

25   I left my place to know them by their name,
Finding them butterfly weed when I came.

The mower in the dew had loved them thus,
By leaving them to flourish, not for us,

Nor yet to draw one thought of ours to him.
30   But from sheer morning gladness at the brim.

The butterfly and I had lit upon,
Nevertheless, a message from the dawn,

That made me hear the wakening birds around,
And hear his long scythe whispering to the ground,

35   And feel a spirit kindred to my own;
So that henceforth I worked no more alone;

But glad with him, I worked as with his aid,
And weary, sought at noon with him the shade;

And dreaming, as it were, held brotherly speech
40   With one whose thought I had not hoped to reach.

"Men work together," I told him from the heart,
"Whether they work together or apart."

Now Close the Windows

Now close the windows and hush all the fields;
   If the trees must, let them silently toss;
No bird is singing now, and if there is,
   Be it my loss.

5   It will be long ere the marshes resume,
   It will be long ere the earliest bird:
So close the windows and not hear the wind,
   But see all wind-stirred.

Reluctance

Out through the fields and the woods
   And over the walls I have wended;
I have climbed the hills of view
   And looked at the world, and descended;
5 I have come by the highway home,
   And lo, it is ended.

The leaves are all dead on the ground,
   Save those that the oak is keeping
To ravel them one by one
10   And let them go scraping and creeping
Out over the crusted snow,
   When others are sleeping.

And the dead leaves lie huddled and still,
   No longer blown hither and thither;
15 The last lone aster is gone;
   The flowers of the witch-hazel wither;
The heart is still aching to seek,
   But the feet question "Whither?"

Ah, when to the heart of man
20   Was it ever less than a treason
To go with the drift of things,
   To yield with a grace to reason,
And bow and accept the end
   Of a love or a season?

FROM

North of Boston

(1914)

The Pasture

I'm going out to clean the pasture spring;
I'll only stop to rake the leaves away
(And wait to watch the water clear, I may):
I sha'n't be gone long.—You come too.

5 I'm going out to fetch the little calf
That's standing by the mother. It's so young,
It totters when she licks it with her tongue.
I sha'n't be gone long.—You come too.

Mending Wall

Something there is that doesn't love a wall,
That sends the frozen-ground-swell under it,
And spills the upper boulders in the sun;
And makes gaps even two can pass abreast.
5 The work of hunters is another thing:
I have come after them and made repair
Where they have left not one stone on stone,
But they would have the rabbit out of hiding,
To please the yelping dogs. The gaps I mean,
10 No one has seen them made or heard them made,
But at spring mending-time we find them there.
I let my neighbour know beyond the hill;
And on a day we meet to walk the line
And set the wall between us once again.
15 We keep the wall between us as we go.
To each the boulders that have fallen to each.
And some are loaves and some so nearly balls
We have to use a spell to make them balance:
"Stay where you are until our backs are turned!"
20 We wear our fingers rough with handling them.
Oh, just another kind of out-door game,
One on a side. It comes to little more:
There where it is we do not need the wall:
He is all pine and I am apple orchard.
25 My apple trees will never get across
And eat the cones under his pines, I tell him.
He only says, "Good fences make good neighbours."
Spring is the mischief in me, and I wonder

If I could put a notion in his head:
30 "*Why* do they make good neighbours? Isn't it
    Where there are cows? But here there are no cows.
    Before I built a wall I'd ask to know
    What I was walling in or walling out,
    And to whom I was like to give offence.
35 Something there is that doesn't love a wall,
    That wants it down." I could say "Elves" to him,
    But it's not elves exactly, and I'd rather
    He said it for himself. I see him there
    Bringing a stone grasped firmly by the top
40 In each hand, like an old-stone savage armed.
    He moves in darkness as it seems to me,
    Not of woods only and the shade of trees.
    He will not go behind his father's saying,
    And he likes having thought of it so well
45 He says again, "Good fences make good neighbours."

The Death of the Hired Man

Mary sat musing on the lamp-flame at the table
Waiting for Warren. When she heard his step,
She ran on tip-toe down the darkened passage
To meet him in the doorway with the news
5 And put him on his guard. "Silas is back."
She pushed him outward with her through the door
And shut it after her. "Be kind," she said.
She took the market things from Warren's arms
And set them on the porch, then drew him down
10 To sit beside her on the wooden steps.

"When was I ever anything but kind to him?
But I'll not have the fellow back," he said.
"I told him so last haying, didn't I?
If he left then, I said, that ended it.
15 What good is he? Who else will harbour him
At his age for the little he can do?
What help he is there's no depending on.
Off he goes always when I need him most.
He thinks he ought to earn a little pay,
20 Enough at least to buy tobacco with,
So he won't have to beg and be beholden.
'All right,' I say, 'I can't afford to pay
Any fixed wages, though I wish I could.'
'Someone else can.' 'Then someone else will have to.'
25 I shouldn't mind his bettering himself
If that was what it was. You can be certain,
When he begins like that, there's someone at him

Trying to coax him off with pocket-money,—
In haying time, when any help is scarce.
30 In winter he comes back to us. I'm done."

"Sh! not so loud: he'll hear you," Mary said.

"I want him to: he'll have to soon or late."

"He's worn out. He's asleep beside the stove.
When I came up from Rowe's I found him here,
35 Huddled against the barn-door fast asleep,
A miserable sight, and frightening, too—
You needn't smile—I didn't recognise him—
I wasn't looking for him—and he's changed.
Wait till you see."

                    "Where did you say he'd been?"

40 "He didn't say. I dragged him to the house,
And gave him tea and tried to make him smoke.
I tried to make him talk about his travels.
Nothing would do: he just kept nodding off."

"What did he say? Did he say anything?"

45 "But little."

              "Anything? Mary, confess
He said he'd come to ditch the meadow for me."

"Warren!"

                    "But did he? I just want to know."

"Of course he did. What would you have him say?
Surely you wouldn't grudge the poor old man
50   Some humble way to save his self-respect.
He added, if you really care to know,
He meant to clear the upper pasture, too.
That sounds like something you have heard before?
Warren, I wish you could have heard the way
55   He jumbled everything. I stopped to look
Two or three times—he made me feel so queer—
To see if he was talking in his sleep.
He ran on Harold Wilson—you remember—
The boy you had in haying four years since.
60   He's finished school, and teaching in his college.
Silas declares you'll have to get him back.
He says they two will make a team for work:
Between them they will lay this farm as smooth!
The way he mixed that in with other things.
65   He thinks young Wilson a likely lad, though daft
On education—you know how they fought
All through July under the blazing sun,
Silas up on the cart to build the load,
Harold along beside to pitch it on."

70   "Yes, I took care to keep well out of earshot."

"Well, those days trouble Silas like a dream.
You wouldn't think they would. How some things linger!
Harold's young college boy's assurance piqued him.
After so many years he still keeps finding
75   Good arguments he sees he might have used.
I sympathise. I know just how it feels
To think of the right thing to say too late.

Harold's associated in his mind with Latin.
He asked me what I thought of Harold's saying
80 He studied Latin like the violin
Because he liked it—that an argument!
He said he couldn't make the boy believe
He could find water with a hazel prong—
Which showed how much good school had ever done him.
85 He wanted to go over that. But most of all
He thinks if he could have another chance
To teach him how to build a load of hay——"

"I know, that's Silas' one accomplishment.
He bundles every forkful in its place,
90 And tags and numbers it for future reference,
So he can find and easily dislodge it
In the unloading. Silas does that well.
He takes it out in bunches like big birds' nests.
You never see him standing on the hay
95 He's trying to lift, straining to lift himself."

"He thinks if he could teach him that, he'd be
Some good perhaps to someone in the world.
He hates to see a boy the fool of books.
Poor Silas, so concerned for other folk,
100 And nothing to look backward to with pride,
And nothing to look forward to with hope,
So now and never any different."

Part of a moon was falling down the west,
Dragging the whole sky with it to the hills.
105 Its light poured softly in her lap. She saw
And spread her apron to it. She put out her hand

Among the harp-like morning-glory strings,
Taut with the dew from garden bed to eaves,
As if she played unheard the tenderness
110 That wrought on him beside her in the night.
"Warren," she said, "he has come home to die:
You needn't be afraid he'll leave you this time."

"Home," he mocked gently.

                                    "Yes, what else but home?
It all depends on what you mean by home.
115 Of course he's nothing to us, any more
Than was the hound that came a stranger to us
Out of the woods, worn out upon the trail."

"Home is the place where, when you have to go there,
They have to take you in."

                              "I should have called it
120 Something you somehow haven't to deserve."

Warren leaned out and took a step or two,
Picked up a little stick, and brought it back
And broke it in his hand and tossed it by.
"Silas has better claim on us you think
125 Than on his brother? Thirteen little miles
As the road winds would bring him to his door.
Silas has walked that far no doubt to-day.
Why didn't he go there? His brother's rich,
A somebody—director in the bank."

130 "He never told us that."

"We know it though."

"I think his brother ought to help, of course.
I'll see to that if there is need. He ought of right
To take him in, and might be willing to—
He may be better than appearances.
135   But have some pity on Silas. Do you think
If he'd had any pride in claiming kin
Or anything he looked for from his brother,
He'd keep so still about him all this time?"

"I wonder what's between them."

                              "I can tell you.
140   Silas is what he is—we wouldn't mind him—
But just the kind that kinsfolk can't abide.
He never did a thing so very bad.
He don't know why he isn't quite as good
As anyone. He won't be made ashamed
145   To please his brother, worthless though he is."

"*I* can't think Si ever hurt anyone."

"No, but he hurt my heart the way he lay
And rolled his old head on that sharp-edged chair-back.
He wouldn't let me put him on the lounge.
150   You must go in and see what you can do.
I made the bed up for him there to-night.
You'll be surprised at him—how much he's broken.
His working days are done; I'm sure of it."

"I'd not be in a hurry to say that."

155   "I haven't been. Go, look, see for yourself.
       But, Warren, please remember how it is:
       He's come to help you ditch the meadow.
       He has a plan. You mustn't laugh at him.
       He may not speak of it, and then he may.
160   I'll sit and see if that small sailing cloud
       Will hit or miss the moon."

                                    It hit the moon.
       Then there were three there, making a dim row,
       The moon, the little silver cloud, and she.

       Warren returned—too soon, it seemed to her,
165   Slipped to her side, caught up her hand and waited.

       "Warren," she questioned.

                                    "Dead," was all he answered.

The Mountain

The mountain held the town as in a shadow.
I saw so much before I slept there once:
I noticed that I missed stars in the west,
Where its black body cut into the sky.
5 Near me it seemed: I felt it like a wall
Behind which I was sheltered from a wind.
And yet between the town and it I found,
When I walked forth at dawn to see new things,
Were fields, a river, and beyond, more fields.
10 The river at the time was fallen away,
And made a widespread brawl on cobble-stones;
But the signs showed what it had done in spring;
Good grass-land gullied out, and in the grass
Ridges of sand, and driftwood stripped of bark.
15 I crossed the river and swung round the mountain.
And there I met a man who moved so slow
With white-faced oxen in a heavy cart,
It seemed no harm to stop him altogether.

"What town is this?" I asked.

                                    "This? Lunenburg."

20 Then I was wrong: the town of my sojourn,
Beyond the bridge, was not that of the mountain,
But only felt at night its shadowy presence.
"Where is your village? Very far from here?"

"There is no village—only scattered farms.
25   We were but sixty voters last election.
We can't in nature grow to many more:
That thing takes all the room!" He moved his goad.
The mountain stood there to be pointed at.
Pasture ran up the side a little way,
30   And then there was a wall of trees with trunks:
After that only tops of trees, and cliffs
Imperfectly concealed among the leaves.
A dry ravine emerged from under boughs
Into the pasture.

                              "That looks like a path.
35   Is that the way to reach the top from here?—
Not for this morning, but some other time:
I must be getting back to breakfast now."

"I don't advise your trying from this side.
There is no proper path, but those that *have*
40   Been up, I understand, have climbed from Ladd's.
That's five miles back. You can't mistake the place:
They logged it there last winter some way up.
I'd take you, but I'm bound the other way."

"You've never climbed it?"

                              "I've been on the sides
45   Deer-hunting and trout-fishing. There's a brook
That starts up on it somewhere—I've heard say
Right on the top, tip-top—a curious thing.
But what would interest you about the brook,
It's always cold in summer, warm in winter.

50   One of the great sights going is to see
      It steam in winter like an ox's breath,
      Until the bushes all along its banks
      Are inch-deep with the frosty spines and bristles—
      You know the kind. Then let the sun shine on it!"

55   "There ought to be a view around the world
      From such a mountain—if it isn't wooded
      Clear to the top." I saw through leafy screens
      Great granite terraces in sun and shadow,
      Shelves one could rest a knee on getting up—
60   With depths behind him sheer a hundred feet;
      Or turn and sit on and look out and down,
      With little ferns in crevices at his elbow.

      "As to that I can't say. But there's the spring,
      Right on the summit, almost like a fountain.
65   That ought to be worth seeing."

                         "If it's there.
      You never saw it?"

                    "I guess there's no doubt
      About its being there. I never saw it.
      It may not be right on the very top:
      It wouldn't have to be a long way down
70   To have some head of water from above,
      And a *good distance* down might not be noticed
      By anyone who'd come a long way up.
      One time I asked a fellow climbing it
      To look and tell me later how it was."

75   "What did he say?"

                              "He said there was a lake
Somewhere in Ireland on a mountain top."

"But a lake's different. What about the spring?"

"He never got up high enough to see.
That's why I don't advise your trying this side.
80   He tried this side. I've always meant to go
And look myself, but you know how it is:
It doesn't seem so much to climb a mountain
You've worked around the foot of all your life.
What would I do? Go in my overalls,
85   With a big stick, the same as when the cows
Haven't come down to the bars at milking time?
Or with a shotgun for a stray black bear?
'Twouldn't seem real to climb for climbing it."

"I shouldn't climb it if I didn't want to—
90   Not for the sake of climbing. What's its name?"

"We call it Hor: I don't know if that's right."

"Can one walk around it? Would it be too far?"

"You can drive round and keep in Lunenburg,
But it's as much as you can ever do,
95   The boundary lines keep in so close to it.
Hor is the township, and the township's Hor—
And a few houses sprinkled round the foot,
Like boulders broken off the upper cliff,
Rolled out a little farther than the rest."

100   "Warm in December, cold in June, you say?"

      "I don't suppose the water's changed at all.
      You and I know enough to know it's warm
      Compared with cold, and cold compared with warm.
      But all the fun's in how you say a thing."

105   "You've lived here all your life?"

                              "Ever since Hor
      Was no bigger than a——" What, I did not hear.
      He drew the oxen toward him with light touches
      Of his slim goad on nose and offside flank,
      Gave them their marching orders and was moving.

Home Burial

He saw her from the bottom of the stairs
Before she saw him. She was starting down,
Looking back over her shoulder at some fear.
She took a doubtful step and then undid it
5   To raise herself and look again. He spoke
Advancing toward her: "What is it you see
From up there always—for I want to know."
She turned and sank upon her skirts at that,
And her face changed from terrified to dull.
10   He said to gain time: "What is it you see,"
Mounting until she cowered under him.
"I will find out now—you must tell me, dear."
She, in her place, refused him any help
With the least stiffening of her neck and silence.
15   She let him look, sure that he wouldn't see,
Blind creature; and a while he didn't see.
But at last he murmured, "Oh," and again, "Oh."

"What is it—what?" she said.

                                        "Just that I see."

"You don't," she challenged. "Tell me what it is."

20   "The wonder is I didn't see at once.
I never noticed it from here before.
I must be wonted to it—that's the reason.
The little graveyard where my people are!

So small the window frames the whole of it.
25   Not so much larger than a bedroom, is it?
There are three stones of slate and one of marble,
Broad-shouldered little slabs there in the sunlight
On the sidehill. We haven't to mind *those*.
But I understand: it is not the stones,
30   But the child's mound——"

                "Don't, don't, don't, don't," she cried.

She withdrew shrinking from beneath his arm
That rested on the banister, and slid downstairs;
And turned on him with such a daunting look,
He said twice over before he knew himself:
35   "Can't a man speak of his own child he's lost?"

"Not you! Oh, where's my hat? Oh, I don't need it!
I must get out of here. I must get air.
I don't know rightly whether any man can."

"Amy! Don't go to someone else this time.
40   Listen to me. I won't come down the stairs."
He sat and fixed his chin between his fists.
"There's something I should like to ask you, dear."

"You don't know how to ask it."

                        "Help me, then."
Her fingers moved the latch for all reply.

45   "My words are nearly always an offence.
I don't know how to speak of anything
So as to please you. But I might be taught

I should suppose. I can't say I see how.
A man must partly give up being a man
50 With women-folk. We could have some arrangement
By which I'd bind myself to keep hands off
Anything special you're a-mind to name.
Though I don't like such things 'twixt those that love.
Two that don't love can't live together without them.
55 But two that do can't live together with them."
She moved the latch a little. "Don't—don't go.
Don't carry it to someone else this time.
Tell me about it if it's something human.
Let me into your grief. I'm not so much
60 Unlike other folks as your standing there
Apart would make me out. Give me my chance.
I do think, though, you overdo it a little.
What was it brought you up to think it the thing
To take your mother-loss of a first child
65 So inconsolably—in the face of love.
You'd think his memory might be satisfied——"

"There you go sneering now!"

                              "I'm not, I'm not!
You make me angry. I'll come down to you.
God, what a woman! And it's come to this,
70 A man can't speak of his own child that's dead."

"You can't because you don't know how.
If you had any feelings, you that dug
With your own hand—how could you?—his little grave;
I saw you from that very window there,
75 Making the gravel leap and leap in air,
Leap up, like that, like that, and land so lightly

And roll back down the mound beside the hole.
I thought, Who is that man? I didn't know you.
And I crept down the stairs and up the stairs
80 To look again, and still your spade kept lifting.
Then you came in. I heard your rumbling voice
Out in the kitchen, and I don't know why,
But I went near to see with my own eyes.
You could sit there with the stains on your shoes
85 Of the fresh earth from your own baby's grave
And talk about your everyday concerns.
You had stood the spade up against the wall
Outside there in the entry, for I saw it."

"I shall laugh the worst laugh I ever laughed.
90 I'm cursed. God, if I don't believe I'm cursed."

"I can repeat the very words you were saying.
'Three foggy mornings and one rainy day
Will rot the best birch fence a man can build.'
Think of it, talk like that at such a time!
95 What had how long it takes a birch to rot
To do with what was in the darkened parlour.
You *couldn't* care! The nearest friends can go
With anyone to death, comes so far short
They might as well not try to go at all.
100 No, from the time when one is sick to death,
One is alone, and he dies more alone.
Friends make pretence of following to the grave,
But before one is in it, their minds are turned
And making the best of their way back to life
105 And living people, and things they understand.
But the world's evil. I won't have grief so
If I can change it. Oh, I won't, I won't!"

"There, you have said it all and you feel better.
You won't go now. You're crying. Close the door.
110   The heart's gone out of it: why keep it up.
Amy! There's someone coming down the road!"

"*You*—oh, you think the talk is all. I must go—
Somewhere out of this house. How can I make you—"

"If—you—do!" She was opening the door wider.
115   "Where do you mean to go? First tell me that.
I'll follow and bring you back by force. I *will!*—"

The Black Cottage

We chanced in passing by that afternoon
To catch it in a sort of special picture
Among tar-banded ancient cherry trees,
Set well back from the road in rank lodged grass,
5   The little cottage we were speaking of,
A front with just a door between two windows,
Fresh painted by the shower a velvet black.
We paused, the minister and I, to look.
He made as if to hold it at arm's length
10 Or put the leaves aside that framed it in.
"Pretty," he said. "Come in. No one will care."
The path was a vague parting in the grass
That led us to a weathered window-sill.
We pressed our faces to the pane. "You see," he said,
15 "Everything's as she left it when she died.
Her sons won't sell the house or the things in it.
They say they mean to come and summer here
Where they were boys. They haven't come this year.
They live so far away—one is out west—
20 It will be hard for them to keep their word.
Anyway they won't have the place disturbed."
A buttoned hair-cloth lounge spread scrolling arms
Under a crayon portrait on the wall
Done sadly from an old daguerreotype.
25 "That was the father as he went to war.
She always, when she talked about war,
Sooner or later came and leaned, half knelt
Against the lounge beside it, though I doubt
If such unlifelike lines kept power to stir

30   Anything in her after all the years.
      He fell at Gettysburg or Fredricksburg,
      I ought to know—it makes a difference which:
      Fredricksburg wasn't Gettysburg, of course.
      But what I'm getting to is how forsaken
35   A little cottage this has always seemed;
      Since she went more than ever, but before—
      I don't mean altogether by the lives
      That had gone out of it, the father first,
      Then the two sons, till she was left alone.
40   (Nothing could draw her after those two sons.
      She valued the considerate neglect
      She had at some cost taught them after years.)
      I mean by the world's having passed it by—
      As we almost got by this afternoon.
45   It always seems to me a sort of mark
      To measure how far fifty years have brought us.
      Why not sit down if you are in no haste?
      These doorsteps seldom have a visitor.
      The warping boards pull out their own old nails
50   With none to tread and put them in their place.
      She had her own idea of things, the old lady.
      And she liked talk. She had seen Garrison
      And Whittier, and had her story of them.
      One wasn't long in learning that she thought
55   Whatever else the Civil War was for
      It wasn't just to keep the States together,
      Nor just to free the slaves, though it did both.
      She wouldn't have believed those ends enough
      To have given outright for them all she gave.
60   Her giving somehow touched the principle
      That all men are created free and equal.
      And to hear her quaint phrases—so removed

From the world's view to-day of all those things.
That's a hard mystery of Jefferson's.
65 What did he mean? Of course the easy way
Is to decide it simply isn't true.
It may not be. I heard a fellow say so.
But never mind, the Welshman got it planted
Where it will trouble us a thousand years.
70 Each age will have to reconsider it.
You couldn't tell her what the West was saying,
And what the South to her serene belief.
She had some art of hearing and yet not
Hearing the latter wisdom of the world.
75 White was the only race she ever knew.
Black she had scarcely seen, and yellow never.
But how could they be made so very unlike
By the same hand working in the same stuff?
She had supposed the war decided that.
80 What are you going to do with such a person?
Strange how such innocence gets its own way.
I shouldn't be surprised if in this world
It were the force that would at last prevail.
Do you know but for her there was a time
85 When to please younger members of the church,
Or rather say non-members in the church,
Whom we all have to think of nowadays,
I would have changed the Creed a very little?
Not that she ever had to ask me not to;
90 It never got so far as that; but the bare thought
Of her old tremulous bonnet in the pew,
And of her half asleep was too much for me.
Why, I might wake her up and startle her.
It was the words 'descended into Hades'
95 That seemed too pagan to our liberal youth.

You know they suffered from a general onslaught.
And well, if they weren't true why keep right on
Saying them like the heathen? We could drop them.
Only—there was the bonnet in the pew.
100   Such a phrase couldn't have meant much to her.
But suppose she had missed it from the Creed
As a child misses the unsaid Good-night,
And falls asleep with heartache—how should *I* feel?
I'm just as glad she made me keep hands off,
105   For, dear me, why abandon a belief
Merely because it ceases to be true.
Cling to it long enough, and not a doubt
It will turn true again, for so it goes.
Most of the change we think we see in life
110   Is due to truths being in and out of favour.
As I sit here, and often times, I wish
I could be monarch of a desert land
I could devote and dedicate forever
To the truths we keep coming back and back to.
115   So desert it would have to be, so walled
By mountain ranges half in summer snow,
No one would covet it or think it worth
The pains of conquering to force change on.
Scattered oases where men dwelt, but mostly
120   Sand dunes held loosely in tamarisk
Blown over and over themselves in idleness.
Sand grains should sugar in the natal dew
The babe born to the desert, the sand storm
Retard mid-waste my cowering caravans—

125   There are bees in this wall." He struck the clapboards,
Fierce heads looked out; small bodies pivoted.
We rose to go. Sunset blazed on the windows.

A Servant to Servants

I didn't make you know how glad I was
To have you come and camp here on our land.
I promised myself to get down some day
And see the way you lived, but I don't know!
5   With a houseful of hungry men to feed
I guess you'd find. . . . It seems to me
I can't express my feelings any more
Than I can raise my voice or want to lift
My hand (oh, I can lift it when I have to).
10 Did ever you feel so? I hope you never.
It's got so I don't even know for sure
Whether I *am* glad, sorry, or anything.
There's nothing but a voice-like left inside
That seems to tell me how I ought to feel,
15 And would feel if I wasn't all gone wrong.
You take the lake. I look and look at it.
I see it's a fair, pretty sheet of water.
I stand and make myself repeat out loud
The advantages it has, so long and narrow,
20 Like a deep piece of some old running river
Cut short off at both ends. It lies five miles
Straight away through the mountain notch
From the sink window where I wash the plates,
And all our storms come up toward the house,
25 Drawing the slow waves whiter and whiter and whiter.
It took my mind off doughnuts and soda biscuit
To step outdoors and take the water dazzle
A sunny morning, or take the rising wind

About my face and body and through my wrapper,
30 When a storm threatened from the Dragon's Den,
And a cold chill shivered across the lake.
I see it's a fair, pretty sheet of water,
Our Willoughby! How did you hear of it?
I expect, though, everyone's heard of it.
35 In a book about ferns? Listen to that!
You let things more like feathers regulate
Your going and coming. And you like it here?
I can see how you might. But I don't know!
It would be different if more people came,
40 For then there would be business. As it is,
The cottages Len built, sometimes we rent them,
Sometimes we don't. We've a good piece of shore
That ought to be worth something, and may yet.
But I don't count on it as much as Len.
45 He looks on the bright side of everything,
Including me. He thinks I'll be all right
With doctoring. But it's not medicine—
Lowe is the only doctor's dared to say so—
It's rest I want—there, I have said it out—
50 From cooking meals for hungry hired men
And washing dishes after them—from doing
Things over and over that just won't stay done.
By good rights I ought not to have so much
Put on me, but there seems no other way.
55 Len says one steady pull more ought to do it.
He says the best way out is always through.
And I agree to that, or in so far
As that I can see no way out but through—
Leastways for me—and then they'll be convinced.
60 It's not that Len don't want the best for me.
It was his plan our moving over in

Beside the lake from where that day I showed you
We used to live—ten miles from anywhere.
We didn't change without some sacrifice,
65 But Len went at it to make up the loss.
His work's a man's, of course, from sun to sun,
But he works when he works as hard as I do—
Though there's small profit in comparisons.
(Women and men will make them all the same.)
70 But work ain't all. Len undertakes too much.
He's into everything in town. This year
It's highways, and he's got too many men
Around him to look after that make waste.
They take advantage of him shamefully,
75 And proud, too, of themselves for doing so.
We have four here to board, great good-for-nothings,
Sprawling about the kitchen with their talk
While I fry their bacon. Much they care!
No more put out in what they do or say
80 Than if I wasn't in the room at all.
Coming and going all the time, they are:
I don't learn what their names are, let alone
Their characters, or whether they are safe
To have inside the house with doors unlocked.
85 I'm not afraid of them, though, if they're not
Afraid of me. There's two can play at that.
I have my fancies: it runs in the family.
My father's brother wasn't right. They kept him
Locked up for years back there at the old farm.
90 I've been away once—yes, I've been away.
The State Asylum. I was prejudiced;
I wouldn't have sent anyone of mine there;
You know the old idea—the only asylum
Was the poorhouse, and those who could afford,

95 Rather than send their folks to such a place,
    Kept them at home; and it does seem more human.
    But it's not so: the place is the asylum.
    There they have every means proper to do with,
    And you aren't darkening other people's lives—
100 Worse than no good to them, and they no good
    To you in your condition; you can't know
    Affection or the want of it in that state.
    I've heard too much of the old-fashioned way.
    My father's brother, he went mad quite young.
105 Some thought he had been bitten by a dog,
    Because his violence took on the form
    Of carrying his pillow in his teeth;
    But it's more likely he was crossed in love,
    Or so the story goes. It was some girl.
110 Anyway all he talked about was love.
    They soon saw he would do someone a mischief
    If he wa'n't kept strict watch of, and it ended
    In father's building him a sort of cage,
    Or room within a room, of hickory poles,
115 Like stanchions in the barn, from floor to ceiling,—
    A narrow passage all the way around.
    Anything they put in for furniture
    He'd tear to pieces, even a bed to lie on.
    So they made the place comfortable with straw,
120 Like a beast's stall, to ease their consciences.
    Of course they had to feed him without dishes.
    They tried to keep him clothed, but he paraded
    With his clothes on his arm—all of his clothes.
    Cruel—it sounds. I 'spose they did the best
125 They knew. And just when he was at the height,
    Father and mother married, and mother came,
    A bride, to help take care of such a creature,

And accommodate her young life to his.
That was what marrying father meant to her.
130 She had to lie and hear love things made dreadful
By his shouts in the night. He'd shout and shout
Until the strength was shouted out of him,
And his voice died down slowly from exhaustion.
He'd pull his bars apart like bow and bow-string,
135 And let them go and make them twang until
His hands had worn them smooth as any ox-bow.
And then he'd crow as if he thought that child's play—
The only fun he had. I've heard them say, though,
They found a way to put a stop to it.
140 He was before my time—I never saw him;
But the pen stayed exactly as it was
There in the upper chamber in the ell,
A sort of catch-all full of attic clutter.
I often think of the smooth hickory bars.
145 It got so I would say—you know, half fooling—
"It's time I took my turn upstairs in jail"—
Just as you will till it becomes a habit.
No wonder I was glad to get away.
Mind you, I waited till Len said the word.
150 I didn't want the blame if things went wrong.
I was glad though, no end, when we moved out,
And I looked to be happy, and I was,
As I said, for a while—but I don't know!
Somehow the change wore out like a prescription.
155 And there's more to it than just window-views
And living by a lake. I'm past such help—
Unless Len took the notion, which he won't,
And I won't ask him—it's not sure enough.
I 'spose I've got to go the road I'm going:
160 Other folks have to, and why shouldn't I?

I almost think if I could do like you,
Drop everything and live out on the ground—
But it might be, come night, I shouldn't like it,
Or a long rain. I should soon get enough,
165 And be glad of a good roof overhead.
I've lain awake thinking of you, I'll warrant,
More than you have yourself, some of these nights.
The wonder was the tents weren't snatched away
From over you as you lay in your beds.
170 I haven't courage for a risk like that.
Bless you, of course you're keeping me from work,
But the thing of it is, I need to *be* kept.
There's work enough to do—there's always that;
But behind's behind. The worst that you can do
175 Is set me back a little more behind.
I shan't catch up in this world, anyway.
I'd *rather* you'd not go unless you must.

After Apple-Picking

My long two-pointed ladder's sticking through a tree
Toward heaven still,
And there's a barrel that I didn't fill
Beside it, and there may be two or three
5   Apples I didn't pick upon some bough.
But I am done with apple-picking now.
Essence of winter sleep is on the night,
The scent of apples: I am drowsing off.
I cannot rub the strangeness from my sight
10 I got from looking through a pane of glass
I skimmed this morning from the drinking trough
And held against the world of hoary grass.
It melted, and I let it fall and break.
But I was well
15 Upon my way to sleep before it fell,
And I could tell
What form my dreaming was about to take.
Magnified apples appear and disappear,
Stem end and blossom end,
20 And every fleck of russet showing clear.
My instep arch not only keeps the ache,
It keeps the pressure of a ladder-round.
I feel the ladder sway as the boughs bend.
And I keep hearing from the cellar bin
25 The rumbling sound
Of load on load of apples coming in.
For I have had too much
Of apple-picking: I am overtired

Of the great harvest I myself desired.
30   There were ten thousand thousand fruit to touch,
Cherish in hand, lift down, and not let fall.
For all
That struck the earth,
No matter if not bruised or spiked with stubble,
35   Went surely to the cider-apple heap
As of no worth.
One can see what will trouble
This sleep of mine, whatever sleep it is.
Were he not gone,
40   The woodchuck could say whether it's like his
Long sleep, as I describe its coming on,
Or just some human sleep.

The Code

There were three in the meadow by the brook
Gathering up windrows, piling cocks of hay,
With an eye always lifted toward the west
Where an irregular sun-bordered cloud
5 Darkly advanced with a perpetual dagger
Flickering across its bosom. Suddenly
One helper, thrusting pitchfork in the ground,
Marched himself off the field and home. One stayed.
The town-bred farmer failed to understand.

10 "What is there wrong?"

                    "Something you just now said."

"What did I say?"

                    "About our taking pains."

"To cock the hay?—because it's going to shower?
I said that more than half an hour ago.
I said it to myself as much as you."

15 "You didn't know. But James is one big fool.
He thought you meant to find fault with his work.
That's what the average farmer would have meant.
James would take time, of course, to chew it over
Before he acted: he's just got round to act."

20 "He is a fool if that's the way he takes me."

"Don't let it bother you. You've found out something.
The hand that knows his business won't be told
To do work better or faster—those two things.
I'm as particular as any one:

25 Most likely I'd have served you just the same.
But I know you don't understand our ways.
You were just talking what was in your mind,
What was in all our minds, and you weren't hinting.
Tell you a story of what happened once:

30 I was up here in Salem at a man's
Named Sanders with a gang of four or five
Doing the haying. No one liked the boss.
He was one of the kind sports call a spider,
All wiry arms and legs that spread out wavy

35 From a humped body nigh as big's a biscuit.
But work! that man could work, especially
If by so doing he could get more work
Out of his hired help. I'm not denying
He was hard on himself. I couldn't find

40 That he kept any hours—not for himself.
Daylight and lantern-light were one to him:
I've heard him pounding in the barn all night.
But what he liked was someone to encourage.
Them that he couldn't lead he'd get behind

45 And drive, the way you can, you know, in mowing—
Keep at their heels and threaten to mow their legs off.
I'd seen about enough of his bulling tricks
(We call that bulling). I'd been watching him.
So when he paired off with me in the hayfield

50 To load the load, thinks I, Look out for trouble.
I built the load and topped it off; old Sanders
Combed it down with a rake and says, 'O.K.'
Everything went well till we reached the barn

With a big catch to empty in a bay.
55 You understand that meant the easy job
For the man up on top of throwing *down*
The hay and rolling it off wholesale,
Where on a mow it would have been slow lifting.
You wouldn't think a fellow'd need much urging
60 Under these circumstances, would you now?
But the old fool seizes his fork in both hands,
And looking up bewhiskered out of the pit,
Shouts like an army captain, 'Let her come!'
Thinks I, D'ye mean it? 'What was that you said?'
65 I asked out loud, so's there'd be no mistake,
'Did you say, Let her come?' 'Yes, let her come.'
He said it over, but he said it softer.
Never you say a thing like that to a man,
Not if he values what he is. God, I'd as soon
70 Murdered him as left out his middle name.
I'd built the load and knew right where to find it.
Two or three forkfuls I picked lightly round for
Like meditating, and then I just dug in
And dumped the rackful on him in ten lots.
75 I looked over the side once in the dust
And caught sight of him treading-water-like,
Keeping his head above. 'Damn ye,' I says,
'That gets ye!' He squeaked like a squeezed rat.
That was the last I saw or heard of him.
80 I cleaned the rack and drove out to cool off.
As I sat mopping hayseed from my neck,
And sort of waiting to be asked about it,
One of the boys sings out, 'Where's the old man?'
'I left him in the barn under the hay.
85 If ye want him, ye can go and dig him out.'
They realized from the way I swobbed my neck

More than was needed something must be up.
They headed for the barn; I stayed where I was.
They told me afterward. First they forked hay,
90   A lot of it, out into the barn floor.
Nothing! They listened for him. Not a rustle.
I guess they thought I'd spiked him in the temple
Before I buried him, or I couldn't have managed.
They excavated more. 'Go keep his wife
95   Out of the barn.' Someone looked in a window,
And curse me if he wasn't in the kitchen
Slumped way down in a chair, with both his feet
Stuck in the oven, the hottest day that summer.
He looked so clean disgusted from behind
100   There was no one that dared to stir him up,
Or let him know that he was being looked at.
Apparently I hadn't buried him
(I may have knocked him down); but my just trying
To bury him had hurt his dignity.
105   He had gone to the house so's not to meet me.
He kept away from us all afternoon.
We tended to his hay. We saw him out
After a while picking peas in his garden:
He couldn't keep away from doing something."

110   "Weren't you relieved to find he wasn't dead?"

      "No! and yet I don't know—it's hard to say.
      I went about to kill him fair enough."

      "You took an awkward way. Did he discharge you?"

      "Discharge me? No! He knew I did just right."

The Housekeeper

I let myself in at the kitchen door.

"It's you," *she said.* "I can't get up. Forgive me
Not answering your knock. I can no more
Let people in than I can keep them out.
5   I'm getting too old for my size, I tell them.
My fingers are about all I've the use of
So's to take any comfort. I can sew:
I help out with this beadwork what I can."

"That's a smart pair of pumps you're beading there.
10 Who are they for?"

                            "You mean?—oh, for some miss.
I can't keep track of other people's daughters.
Lord, if I were to dream of everyone
Whose shoes I primped to dance in!"

                                        "And where's John?"

"Haven't you seen him? Strange what set you off
15 To come to his house when he's gone to yours.
You can't have passed each other. I know what:
He must have changed his mind and gone to Garland's.
He won't be long in that case. You can wait.
Though what good you can be, or anyone—
20 It's gone so far. You've heard? Estelle's run off."

"Yes, what's it all about? When did she go?"

"Two weeks since."

                    "She's in earnest, it appears."

"I'm sure she won't come back. She's hiding somewhere.
I don't know where myself. John thinks I do.
25 He thinks I only have to say the word,
And she'll come back. But, bless you, I'm her mother—
I can't talk to her, and, Lord, if I could!"

"It will go hard with John. What will he do?
He can't find anyone to take her place."

30 "Oh, if you ask me that, what *will* he do?
He gets some sort of bakeshop meals together,
With me to sit and tell him everything,
What's wanted and how much and where it is.
But when I'm gone—of course I can't stay here:
35 Estelle's to take me when she's settled down.
He and I only hinder one another.
I tell them they can't get me through the door, though:
I've been built in here like a big church organ.
We've been here fifteen years."

                              "That's a long time
40 To live together and then pull apart.
How do you see him living when you're gone?
Two of you out will leave an empty house."

"I don't just see him living many years,
Left here with nothing but the furniture.

45 I hate to think of the old place when we're gone,
   With the brook going by below the yard,
   And no one here but hens blowing about.
   If he could sell the place, but then, he can't:
   No one will ever live on it again.
50 It's too run down. This is the last of it.
   What I think he will do, is let things smash.
   He'll sort of swear the time away. He's awful!
   I never saw a man let family troubles
   Make so much difference in his man's affairs.
55 He's just dropped everything. He's like a child.
   I blame his being brought up by his mother.
   He's got hay down that's been rained on three times.
   He hoed a little yesterday for me:
   I thought the growing things would do him good.
60 Something went wrong. I saw him throw the hoe
   Sky-high with both hands. I can see it now—
   Come here—I'll show you—in that apple tree.
   That's no way for a man to do at his age:
   He's fifty-five, you know, if he's a day."

65 "Aren't you afraid of him? What's that gun for?"

   "Oh, that's been there for hawks since chicken-time.
   John Hall touch me! Not if he knows his friends.
   I'll say that for him, John's no threatener
   Like some men folk. No one's afraid of him;
70 All is, he's made up his mind not to stand
   What he has got to stand."

                        "Where is Estelle?
   Couldn't one talk to her? What does she say?

You say you don't know where she is."

                                    "Nor want to!
She thinks if it was bad to live with him,
75   It must be right to leave him."

                          "Which is wrong!"

"Yes, but he should have married her."

                                  "I know."

"The strain's been too much for her all these years:
I can't explain it any other way.
It's different with a man, at least with John:
80   He knows he's kinder than the run of men.
Better than married ought to be as good
As married—that's what he has always said.
I know the way he's felt—but all the same!"

"I wonder why he doesn't marry her
85   And end it."

                 "Too late now: she wouldn't have him.
He's given her time to think of something else.
That's his mistake. The dear knows my interest
Has been to keep the thing from breaking up.
This is a good home: I don't ask for better.
90   But when I've said, 'Why shouldn't they be married,'
He'd say, 'Why should they?' no more words than that."

"And after all why should they? John's been fair

I take it. What was his was always hers.
There was no quarrel about property."

95 "Reason enough, there was no property.
A friend or two as good as own the farm,
Such as it is. It isn't worth the mortgage."

"I mean Estelle has always held the purse."

"The rights of that are harder to get at.
100 I guess Estelle and I have filled the purse.
'Twas we let him have money, not he us.
John's a bad farmer. I'm not blaming him.
Take it year in, year out, he doesn't make much.
We came here for a home for me, you know,
105 Estelle to do the housework for the board
Of both of us. But look how it turns out:
She seems to have the housework, and besides
Half of the outdoor work, though as for that,
He'd say she does it more because she likes it.
110 You see our pretty things are all outdoors.
Our hens and cows and pigs are always better
Than folks like us have any business with.
Farmers around twice as well off as we
Haven't as good. They don't go with the farm.
115 One thing you can't help liking about John,
He's fond of nice things—too fond, some would say.
But Estelle don't complain: she's like him there.
She wants our hens to be the best there are.
You never saw this room before a show,
120 Full of lank, shivery, half-drowned birds
In separate coops, having their plumage done.

The smell of the wet feathers in the heat!
You spoke of John's not being safe to stay with.
You don't know what a gentle lot we are:
125   We wouldn't hurt a hen! You ought to see us
Moving a flock of hens from place to place.
We're not allowed to take them upside down,
All we can hold together by the legs.
Two at a time's the rule, one on each arm,
130   No matter how far and how many times
We have to go."

                    "You mean that's John's idea."

      "And we live up to it; or I don't know
What childishness he wouldn't give way to.
He manages to keep the upper hand
135   On his own farm. He's boss. But as to hens:
We fence our flowers in and the hens range.
Nothing's too good for them. We say it pays.
John likes to tell the offers he has had,
Twenty for this cock, twenty-five for that.
140   He never takes the money. If they're worth
That much to sell, they're worth as much to keep.
Bless you, it's all expense, though. Reach me down
The little tin box on the cupboard shelf,
The upper shelf, the tin box. That's the one.
145   I'll show you. Here you are."

                              "What's this?"

                                          "A bill—

For fifty dollars for one Langshang cock—
Receipted. And the cock is in the yard."

"Not in a glass case, then?"

                              "He'd need a tall one:
He can eat off a barrel from the ground.
150 He's been in a glass case, as you may say,
The Crystal Palace, London. He's imported.
John bought him, and we paid the bill with beads—
Wampum, I call it. Mind, we don't complain.
But you see, don't you, we take care of him."

155 "And like it, too. It makes it all the worse."

"It seems as if. And that's not all: he's helpless
In ways that I can hardly tell you of.
Sometimes he gets possessed to keep accounts
To see where all the money goes so fast.
160 You know how men will be ridiculous.
But it's just fun the way he gets bedeviled—
If he's untidy now, what will he be——?"

"It makes it all the worse. You must be blind."

"Estelle's the one. You needn't talk to me."

165 "Can't you and I get to the root of it?
What's the real trouble? What will satisfy her?"

"It's as I say: she's turned from him, that's all."

"But why, when she's well off? Is it the neighbours,
Being cut off from friends?"

                              "We have our friends.

170 That isn't it. Folks aren't afraid of us."

"She's let it worry her. You stood the strain,
And you're her mother."

                      "But I didn't always.
I didn't relish it along at first.
But I got wonted to it. And besides—
175 John said I was too old to have grandchildren.
But what's the use of talking when it's done?
She won't come back—it's worse than that—she can't."

"Why do you speak like that? What do you know?
What do you mean?—she's done harm to herself?"

180 "I mean she's married—married someone else."

"Oho, oho!"

           "You don't believe me."

                        "Yes, I do,
Only too well. I knew there must be something!
So that was what was back. She's bad, that's all!"

"Bad to get married when she had the chance?"

185 "Nonsense! See what she's done! But who, who——"

"Who'd marry her straight out of such a mess?
Say it right out—no matter for her mother.
The man was found. I'd better name no names.
John himself won't imagine who he is."

190   "Then it's all up. I think I'll get away.
You'll be expecting John. I pity Estelle;
I suppose she deserves some pity, too.
You ought to have the kitchen to yourself
To break it to him. You may have the job."

195   "You needn't think you're going to get away.
John's almost here. I've had my eye on someone
Coming down Ryan's Hill. I thought 'twas him.
Here he is now. This box! Put it away.
And this bill."

        "What's the hurry? He'll unhitch."

200   "No, he won't, either. He'll just drop the reins
And turn Doll out to pasture, rig and all.
She won't get far before the wheels hang up
On something—there's no harm. See, there he is!
My, but he looks as if he must have heard!"

205   *John threw the door wide but he didn't enter.*
"How are you, neighbour? Just the man I'm after.
Isn't it Hell," *he said.* "I want to know.
Come out here if you want to hear me talk.
I'll talk to you, old woman, afterward.
210 I've got some news that maybe isn't news.
What are they trying to do to me, these two?"

  "Do go along with him and stop his shouting."
She raised her voice against the closing door:
"Who wants to hear your news, you—dreadful fool?"

The Fear

A lantern light from deeper in the barn
Shone on a man and woman in the door
And threw their lurching shadows on a house
Near by, all dark in every glossy window.
5 A horse's hoof pawed once the hollow floor,
And the back of the gig they stood beside
Moved in a little. The man grasped a wheel,
The woman spoke out sharply, "Whoa, stand still!
I saw it just as plain as a white plate,"
10 She said, "as the light on the dashboard ran
Along the bushes at the roadside—a man's face.
You *must* have seen it too."

                              "I didn't see it.
Are you sure——"

                    "Yes, I'm sure!"

                                        "—it was a face?"

"Joel, I'll have to look. I can't go in,
15 I can't, and leave a thing like that unsettled.
Doors locked and curtains drawn will make no difference.
I always have felt strange when we came home
To the dark house after so long an absence,
And the key rattled loudly into place
20 Seemed to warn someone to be getting out

68

At one door as we entered at another.
What if I'm right, and someone all the time—
Don't hold my arm!"

        "I say it's someone passing."

"You speak as if this were a travelled road.
25   You forget where we are. What is beyond
That he'd be going to or coming from
At such an hour of night, and on foot too.
What was he standing still for in the bushes?"

"It's not so very late—it's only dark.
30   There's more in it than you're inclined to say.
Did he look like——?"

        "He looked like anyone.
I'll never rest to-night unless I know.
Give me the lantern."

        "You don't want the lantern."

She pushed past him and got it for herself.

35   "You're not to come," she said. "This is my business.
If the time's come to face it, I'm the one
To put it the right way. He'd never dare—
Listen! He kicked a stone. Hear that, hear that!
He's coming towards us. Joel, *go* in—please.
40   Hark!—I don't hear him now. But please go in."

"In the first place you can't make me believe it's——"

"It is—or someone else he's sent to watch.
And now's the time to have it out with him
While we know definitely where he is.
45 Let him get off and he'll be everywhere
Around us, looking out of trees and bushes
Till I shan't dare to set a foot outdoors.
And I can't stand it. Joel, let me go!"

"But it's nonsense to think he'd care enough."

50 "You mean you couldn't understand his caring.
Oh, but you see he hadn't had enough—
Joel, I won't—I won't—I promise you.
We mustn't say hard things. You mustn't either."

"I'll be the one, if anybody goes!
55 But you give him the advantage with this light.
What couldn't he do to us standing here!
And if to see was what he wanted, why
He has seen all there was to see and gone."

He appeared to forget to keep his hold,
60 But advanced with her as she crossed the grass.

"What do you want?" she cried to all the dark.
She stretched up tall to overlook the light
That hung in both hands hot against her skirt.

"There's no one; so you're wrong," he said.

                                        "There is.—
65 What do you want?" she cried, and then herself
Was startled when an answer really came.

"Nothing." It came from well along the road.

She reached a hand to Joel for support:
The smell of scorching woollen made her faint.
70 "What are you doing round this house at night?"

"Nothing." A pause: there seemed no more to say.

And then the voice again: "You seem afraid.
I saw by the way you whipped up the horse.
I'll just come forward in the lantern light
75 And let you see."

                    "Yes, do.—Joel, go back!"

She stood her ground against the noisy steps
That came on, but her body rocked a little.

"You see," the voice said.

                    "Oh." She looked and looked.

"You don't see—I've a child here by the hand."

80 "What's a child doing at this time of night——?"

"Out walking. Every child should have the memory
Of at least one long-after-bedtime walk.
What, son?"

                    "Then I should think you'd try to find
Somewhere to walk——"

"The highway as it happens—
85   We're stopping for the fortnight down at Dean's."

"But if that's all—Joel—you realize—
You won't think anything. You understand?
You understand that we have to be careful.
This is a very, very lonely place.
90   Joel!" She spoke as if she couldn't turn.
The swinging lantern lengthened to the ground,
It touched, it struck, it clattered and went out.

The Self-Seeker

"Willis, I didn't want you here to-day:
The lawyer's coming for the company.
I'm going to sell my soul, or, rather, feet.
Five hundred dollars for the pair, you know."

5   "With you the feet have nearly been the soul;
And if you're going to sell them to the devil,
I want to see you do it. When's he coming?"

"I half suspect you knew, and came on purpose
To try to help me drive a better bargain."

10 "Well, if it's true! Yours are no common feet.
The lawyer don't know what it is he's buying:
So many miles you might have walked you won't walk.
You haven't run your forty orchids down.
What does he think?—How *are* the blessed feet?
15 The doctor's sure you're going to walk again?"

"He thinks I'll hobble. It's both legs and feet."

"They must be terrible—I mean to look at."

"I haven't dared to look at them uncovered.
Through the bed blankets I remind myself
20 Of a starfish laid out with rigid points."

"The wonder is it hadn't been your head."

"It's hard to tell you how I managed it.
When I saw the shaft had me by the coat,
I didn't try too long to pull away,
25   Or fumble for my knife to cut away,
I just embraced the shaft and rode it out—
Till Weiss shut off the water in the wheel-pit.
That's how I think I didn't lose my head.
But my legs got their knocks against the ceiling."

30   "Awful. Why didn't they throw off the belt
Instead of going clear down in the wheel-pit?"

"They say some time was wasted on the belt—
Old streak of leather—doesn't love me much
Because I make him spit fire at my knuckles,
35   The way Ben Franklin used to make the kite-string.
That must be it. Some days he won't stay on.
That day a woman couldn't coax him off.
He's on his rounds now with his tail in his mouth
Snatched right and left across the silver pulleys.
40   Everything goes the same without me there.
You can hear the small buzz saws whine, the big saw
Caterwaul to the hills around the village
As they both bite the wood. It's all our music.
One ought as a good villager to like it.
45   No doubt it has a sort of prosperous sound,
And it's our life."

                    "Yes, when it's not our death."

"You make that sound as if it wasn't so
With everything. What we live by we die by.
I wonder where my lawyer is. His train's in.
50   I want this over with; I'm hot and tired."

"You're getting ready to do something foolish."

"Watch for him, will you, Will? You let him in.
I'd rather Mrs. Corbin didn't know;
I've boarded here so long, she thinks she owns me.
55   You're bad enough to manage without her."

"And I'm going to be worse instead of better.
You've got to tell me how far this is gone;
Have you agreed to any price?"

                              "Five hundred.
Five hundred—five—five! One, two, three, four, five.
60   You needn't look at me."

                         "I don't believe you."

"I told you, Willis, when you first came in.
Don't you be hard on me. I have to take
What I can get. You see they have the feet,
Which gives them the advantage in the trade.
65   I can't get back the feet in any case."

"But your flowers, man, you're selling out your flowers."

"Yes, that's one way to put it—all the flowers
Of every kind everywhere in this region
For the next forty summers—call it forty.
70   But I'm not selling those, I'm giving them,
They never earned me so much as one cent:
Money can't pay me for the loss of them.
No, the five hundred was the sum they named
To pay the doctor's bill and tide me over.

75   It's that or fight, and I don't want to fight—
     I just want to get settled in my life,
     Such as it's going to be, and know the worst,
     Or best—it may not be so bad. The firm
     Promise me all the shooks I want to nail."

80   "But what about your flora of the valley?"

     "You have me there. But that—you didn't think
     That was worth money to me? Still I own
     It goes against me not to finish it
     For the friends it might bring me. By the way,
85   I had a letter from Burroughs—did I tell you?—
     About my *Cyprepedium reginæ*;
     He says it's not reported so far north.
     There! there's the bell. He's rung. But you go down
     And bring him up, and don't let Mrs. Corbin.—
90   Oh, well, we'll soon be through with it. I'm tired."

     Willis brought up besides the Boston lawyer
     A little barefoot girl who in the noise
     Of heavy footsteps in the old frame house,
     And baritone importance of the lawyer,
95   Stood for a while unnoticed with her hands
     Shyly behind her.

                         "Well, and how is Mister——"

     The lawyer was already in his satchel
     As if for papers that might bear the name
     He hadn't at command. "You must excuse me,
100 I dropped in at the mill and was detained."

     "Looking round, I suppose," said Willis.

                                        "Yes,
Well, yes."

          "Hear anything that might prove useful?"

The Broken One saw Anne. "Why, here is Anne.
What do you want, dear? Come, stand by the bed;
105 Tell me what is it?" Anne just wagged her dress
With both hands held behind her. "Guess," she said.
"Oh, guess which hand? My, my! Once on a time
I knew a lovely way to tell for certain
By looking in the ears. But I forget it.
110 Er, let me see. I think I'll take the right.
That's sure to be right even if it's wrong.
Come, hold it out. Don't change.—A Ram's Horn orchid!
A Ram's Horn! What would I have got, I wonder,
If I had chosen left. Hold out the left.
115 Another Ram's Horn! Where did you find those,
Under what beech tree, on what woodchuck's knoll?"
Anne looked at the large lawyer at her side,
And thought she wouldn't venture on so much.

"Were there no others?"

                              "There were four or five.
120 I knew you wouldn't let me pick them all."

"I wouldn't—so I wouldn't. You're the girl!
You see Anne has her lesson learned by heart."

"I wanted there should be some there next year."

"Of course you did. You left the rest for seed,
125 And for the backwoods woodchuck. You're the girl!

A Ram's Horn orchid seedpod for a woodchuck
Sounds something like. Better than farmer's beans
To a discriminating appetite,
Though the Ram's Horn is seldom to be had
130   In bushel lots—doesn't come on the market.
But, Anne, I'm troubled; have you told me all?
You're hiding something. That's as bad as lying.
You ask this lawyer man. And it's not safe
With a lawyer at hand to find you out.
135   Nothing is hidden from some people, Anne.
You don't tell me that where you found a Ram's Horn
You didn't find a Yellow Lady's Slipper.
What did I tell you? What? I'd blush, I would.
Don't you defend yourself. If it was there,
140   Where is it now, the Yellow Lady's Slipper?"

"Well, wait—it's common—it's too *common*."

                                    "Common?

The Purple Lady's Slipper's commoner."

"I didn't bring a Purple Lady's Slipper
To *You*—to you I mean—they're both too common."

145   The lawyer gave a laugh among his papers
As if with some idea that she had scored.

"I've broken Anne of gathering bouquets.
It's not fair to the child. It can't be helped though:
Pressed into service means pressed out of shape.
150   Somehow I'll make it right with her—she'll see.

She's going to do my scouting in the field,
Over stone walls and all along a wood
And by a river bank for water flowers,
The floating Heart, with small leaf like a heart,
155   And at the *sinus* under water a fist
Of little fingers all kept down but one,
And that thrust up to blossom in the sun
As if to say, 'You! You're the Heart's desire.'
Anne has a way with flowers to take the place
160   Of that she's lost: she goes down on one knee
And lifts their faces by the chin to hers
And says their names, and leaves them where they are."

The lawyer wore a watch the case of which
Was cunningly devised to make a noise
165   Like a small pistol when he snapped it shut
At such a time as this. He snapped it now.

"Well, Anne, go, dearie. Our affair will wait.
The lawyer man is thinking of his train.
He wants to give me lots and lots of money
170   Before he goes, because I hurt myself,
And it may take him I don't know how long.
But put our flowers in water first. Will, help her:
The pitcher's too full for her. There's no cup?
Just hook them on the inside of the pitcher.
175   Now run.—Get out your documents! You see
I have to keep on the good side of Anne.
I'm a great boy to think of number one.
And you can't blame me in the place I'm in.
Who will take care of my necessities
180   Unless I do?"

                        "A pretty interlude,"
The lawyer said. "I'm sorry, but my train—
Luckily terms are all agreed upon.
You only have to sign your name. Right—there."

"You, Will, stop making faces. Come round here
185 Where you can't make them. What is it you want?
I'll put you out with Anne. Be good or go."

"You don't mean you will sign that thing unread?"

"Make yourself useful then, and read it for me.
Isn't it something I have seen before?"

190 "You'll find it is. Let your friend look at it."

"Yes, but all that takes time, and I'm as much
In haste to get it over with as you.
But read it, read it. That's right, draw the curtain:
Half the time I don't know what's troubling me.—
195 What do you say, Will? Don't you be a fool,
You! crumpling folkses legal documents.
Out with it if you've any real objection."

"Five hundred dollars!"

                              "What would you think right?"

"A thousand wouldn't be a cent too much;
200 You know it, Mr. Lawyer. The sin is
Accepting anything before he knows
Whether he's ever going to walk again.
It smells to me like a dishonest trick."

"I think—I think—from what I heard to-day—
205 And saw myself—he would be ill-advised——"

"What did you hear, for instance?" Willis said.

"Now the place where the accident occurred—"

The Broken One was twisted in his bed.
"This is between you two apparently.
210 Where I come in is what I want to know.
You stand up to it like a pair of cocks.
Go outdoors if you want to fight. Spare me.
When you come back, I'll have the papers signed.
Will pencil do? Then, please, your fountain pen.
215 One of you hold my head up from the pillow."

Willis flung off the bed. "I wash my hands—
I'm no match—no, and don't pretend to be——"

The lawyer gravely capped his fountain pen.
"You're doing the wise thing: you won't regret it.
220 We're very sorry for you."

                    Willis sneered:
"Who's *we*?—some stockholders in Boston?
I'll go outdoors, by gad, and won't come back."

"Willis, bring Anne back with you when you come.
Yes. Thanks for caring. Don't mind Will: he's savage.
225 He thinks you ought to pay me for my flowers.
You don't know what I mean about the flowers.
Don't stop to try to now. You'll miss your train.
Good-bye." He flung his arms around his face.

The Wood-Pile

Out walking in the frozen swamp one grey day
I paused and said, "I will turn back from here.
No, I will go on farther—and we shall see."
The hard snow held me, save where now and then
5 One foot went down. The view was all in lines
Straight up and down of tall slim trees
Too much alike to mark or name a place by
So as to say for certain I was here
Or somewhere else: I was just far from home.
10 A small bird flew before me. He was careful
To put a tree between us when he lighted,
And say no word to tell me who he was
Who was so foolish as to think what *he* thought.
He thought that I was after him for a feather—
15 The white one in his tail; like one who takes
Everything said as personal to himself.
One flight out sideways would have undeceived him.
And then there was a pile of wood for which
I forgot him and let his little fear
20 Carry him off the way I might have gone,
Without so much as wishing him good-night.
He went behind it to make his last stand.
It was a cord of maple, cut and split
And piled—and measured, four by four by eight.
25 And not another like it could I see.
No runner tracks in this year's snow looped near it.
And it was older sure than this year's cutting,
Or even last year's or the year's before.

The wood was grey and the bark warping off it
30   And the pile somewhat sunken. Clematis
Had wound strings round and round it like a bundle.
What held it though on one side was a tree
Still growing, and on one a stake and prop,
These latter about to fall. I thought that only
35   Someone who lived in turning to fresh tasks
Could so forget his handiwork on which
He spent himself, the labour of his axe,
And leave it there far from a useful fireplace
To warm the frozen swamp as best it could
40   With the slow smokeless burning of decay.

Good Hours

I had for my winter evening walk—
No one at all with whom to talk,
But I had the cottages in a row
Up to their shining eyes in snow.

5 And I thought I had the folk within:
I had the sound of a violin;
I had a glimpse through curtain laces
Of youthful forms and youthful faces.

I had such company outward bound.
10 I went till there were no cottages found.
I turned and repented, but coming back
I saw no window but that was black.

Over the snow my creaking feet
Disturbed the slumbering village street
15 Like profanation, by your leave,
At ten o'clock of a winter eve.

FROM
Mountain Interval
(1916)

The Road Not Taken

Two roads diverged in a yellow wood,
And sorry I could not travel both
And be one traveler, long I stood
And looked down one as far as I could
5   To where it bent in the undergrowth;

Then took the other, as just as fair,
And having perhaps the better claim,
Because it was grassy and wanted wear;
Though as for that the passing there
10   Had worn them really about the same,

And both that morning equally lay
In leaves no step had trodden black.
Oh, I kept the first for another day!
Yet knowing how way leads on to way,
15   I doubted if I should ever come back.

I shall be telling this with a sigh
Somewhere ages and ages hence:
Two roads diverged in a wood, and I—
I took the one less traveled by,
20   And that has made all the difference.

An Old Man's Winter Night

All out of doors looked darkly in at him
Through the thin frost, almost in separate stars,
That gathers on the pane in empty rooms.
What kept his eyes from giving back the gaze
5   Was the lamp tilted near them in his hand.
What kept him from remembering what it was
That brought him to that creaking room was age.
He stood with barrels round him—at a loss.
And having scared the cellar under him
10 In clomping there, he scared it once again
In clomping off;—and scared the outer night,
Which has its sounds, familiar, like the roar
Of trees and crack of branches, common things,
But nothing so like beating on a box.
15 A light he was to no one but himself
Where now he sat, concerned with he knew what,
A quiet light, and then not even that.
He consigned to the moon, such as she was,
So late-arising, to the broken moon
20 As better than the sun in any case
For such a charge, his snow upon the roof,
His icicles along the wall to keep;
And slept. The log that shifted with a jolt
Once in the stove, disturbed him and he shifted,
25 And eased his heavy breathing, but still slept.
One aged man—one man—can't fill a house,
A farm, a countryside, or if he can,
It's thus he does it of a winter night.

A Patch of Old Snow

There's a patch of old snow in a corner
   That I should have guessed
Was a blow-away paper the rain
   Had brought to rest.

5   It is speckled with grime as if
     Small print overspread it,
The news of a day I've forgotten—
     If I ever read it.

Meeting and Passing

As I went down the hill along the wall
There was a gate I had leaned at for the view
And had just turned from when I first saw you
As you came up the hill. We met. But all
5   We did that day was mingle great and small
Footprints in summer dust as if we drew
The figure of our being less than two
But more than one as yet. Your parasol

Pointed the decimal off with one deep thrust.
10 And all the time we talked you seemed to see
Something down there to smile at in the dust.
(Oh, it was without prejudice to me!)
Afterward I went past what you had passed
Before we met and you what I had passed.

Hyla Brook

By June our brook's run out of song and speed.
Sought for much after that, it will be found
Either to have gone groping underground
(And taken with it all the Hyla breed
5   That shouted in the mist a month ago,
Like ghost of sleigh-bells in a ghost of snow)—
Or flourished and come up in jewel-weed,
Weak foliage that is blown upon and bent
Even against the way its waters went.
10   Its bed is left a faded paper sheet
Of dead leaves stuck together by the heat—
A brook to none but who remember long.
This as it will be seen is other far
Than with brooks taken otherwhere in song.
15   We love the things we love for what they are.

The Oven Bird

There is a singer everyone has heard,
Loud, a mid-summer and a mid-wood bird,
Who makes the solid tree trunks sound again.
He says that leaves are old and that for flowers
5   Mid-summer is to spring as one to ten.
He says the early petal-fall is past
When pear and cherry bloom went down in showers
On sunny days a moment overcast;
And comes that other fall we name the fall.
10   He says the highway dust is over all.
The bird would cease and be as other birds
But that he knows in singing not to sing.
The question that he frames in all but words
Is what to make of a diminished thing.

Bond and Free

Love has earth to which she clings
With hills and circling arms about—
Wall within wall to shut fear out.
But Thought has need of no such things,
5   For Thought has a pair of dauntless wings.

On snow and sand and turf, I see
Where Love has left a printed trace
With straining in the world's embrace.
And such is Love and glad to be.
10   But Thought has shaken his ankles free.

Thought cleaves the interstellar gloom
And sits in Sirius' disc all night,
Till day makes him retrace his flight,
With smell of burning on every plume,
15   Back past the sun to an earthly room.

His gains in heaven are what they are.
Yet some say Love by being thrall
And simply staying possesses all
In several beauty that Thought fares far
20   To find fused in another star.

Birches

When I see birches bend to left and right
Across the lines of straighter darker trees,
I like to think some boy's been swinging them.
But swinging doesn't bend them down to stay.
5 Ice-storms do that. Often you must have seen them
Loaded with ice a sunny winter morning
After a rain. They click upon themselves
As the breeze rises, and turn many-colored
As the stir cracks and crazes their enamel.
10 Soon the sun's warmth makes them shed crystal shells
Shattering and avalanching on the snow-crust—
Such heaps of broken glass to sweep away
You'd think the inner dome of heaven had fallen.
They are dragged to the withered bracken by the load,
15 And they seem not to break; though once they are bowed
So low for long, they never right themselves:
You may see their trunks arching in the woods
Years afterwards, trailing their leaves on the ground
Like girls on hands and knees that throw their hair
20 Before them over their heads to dry in the sun.
But I was going to say when Truth broke in
With all her matter-of-fact about the ice-storm
(Now am I free to be poetical?)
I should prefer to have some boy bend them
25 As he went out and in to fetch the cows—
Some boy too far from town to learn baseball,
Whose only play was what he found himself,
Summer or winter, and could play alone.

One by one he subdued his father's trees
30 By riding them down over and over again
Until he took the stiffness out of them,
And not one but hung limp, not one was left
For him to conquer. He learned all there was
To learn about not launching out too soon
35 And so not carrying the tree away
Clear to the ground. He always kept his poise
To the top branches, climbing carefully
With the same pains you use to fill a cup
Up to the brim, and even above the brim.
40 Then he flung outward, feet first, with a swish,
Kicking his way down through the air to the ground.
So was I once myself a swinger of birches.
And so I dream of going back to be.
It's when I'm weary of considerations,
45 And life is too much like a pathless wood
Where your face burns and tickles with the cobwebs
Broken across it, and one eye is weeping
From a twig's having lashed across it open.
I'd like to get away from earth awhile
50 And then come back to it and begin over.
May no fate willfully misunderstand me
And half grant what I wish and snatch me away
Not to return. Earth's the right place for love:
I don't know where it's likely to go better.
55 I'd like to go by climbing a birch tree,
And climb black branches up a snow-white trunk
Toward heaven, till the tree could bear no more,
But dipped its top and set me down again.
That would be good both going and coming back.
60 One could do worse than be a swinger of birches.

Putting in the Seed

You come to fetch me from my work to-night
When supper's on the table, and we'll see
If I can leave off burying the white
Soft petals fallen from the apple tree.
5   (Soft petals, yes, but not so barren quite,
Mingled with these, smooth bean and wrinkled pea;)
And go along with you ere you lose sight
Of what you came for and become like me,
Slave to a springtime passion for the earth.
10 How Love burns through the Putting in the Seed
On through the watching for that early birth
When, just as the soil tarnishes with weed,

The sturdy seedling with arched body comes
Shouldering its way and shedding the earth crumbs.

The Cow in Apple Time

Something inspires the only cow of late
To make no more of a wall than an open gate,
And think no more of wall-builders than fools.
Her face is flecked with pomace and she drools
5 A cider syrup. Having tasted fruit,
She scorns a pasture withering to the root.
She runs from tree to tree where lie and sweeten
The windfalls spiked with stubble and worm-eaten.
She leaves them bitten when she has to fly.
10 She bellows on a knoll against the sky.
Her udder shrivels and the milk goes dry.

Range-Finding

The battle rent a cobweb diamond-strung
And cut a flower beside a ground bird's nest
Before it stained a single human breast.
The stricken flower bent double and so hung.
5   And still the bird revisited her young.
A butterfly its fall had dispossessed
A moment sought in air his flower of rest,
Then lightly stooped to it and fluttering clung.
On the bare upland pasture there had spread
10 O'ernight 'twixt mullein stalks a wheel of thread
And straining cables wet with silver dew.
A sudden passing bullet shook it dry.
The indwelling spider ran to greet the fly,
But finding nothing, sullenly withdrew.

The Hill Wife

(Her Word)

One ought not to have to care
  So much as you and I
Care when the birds come round the house
  To seem to say good-bye;

5 Or care so much when they come back
    With whatever it is they sing;
The truth being we are as much
  Too glad for the one thing

As we are too sad for the other here—
10   With birds that fill their breasts
But with each other and themselves
  And their built or driven nests.

HOUSE FEAR

Always—I tell you this they learned—
Always at night when they returned
To the lonely house from far away
To lamps unlighted and fire gone gray,
5 They learned to rattle the lock and key
To give whatever might chance to be
Warning and time to be off in flight:
And preferring the out- to the in-door night,

They learned to leave the house-door wide
10   Until they had lit the lamp inside.

THE SMILE

(Her Word)

I didn't like the way he went away.
That smile! It never came of being gay.
Still he smiled—did you see him?—I was sure!
Perhaps because we gave him only bread
5   And the wretch knew from that that we were poor.
Perhaps because he let us give instead
Of seizing from us as he might have seized.
Perhaps he mocked at us for being wed,
Or being very young (and he was pleased
10   To have a vision of us old and dead).
I wonder how far down the road he's got.
He's watching from the woods as like as not.

THE OFT-REPEATED DREAM

She had no saying dark enough
    For the dark pine that kept
Forever trying the window-latch
    Of the room where they slept.

5   The tireless but ineffectual hands
    That with every futile pass
Made the great tree seem as a little bird
    Before the mystery of glass!

It never had been inside the room,
10   And only one of the two

Was afraid in an oft-repeated dream
   Of what the tree might do.

THE IMPULSE

It was too lonely for her there,
   And too wild,
And since there were but two of them,
   And no child,

5 And work was little in the house,
   She was free,
And followed where he furrowed field,
   Or felled tree.

She rested on a log and tossed
10   The fresh chips,
With a song only to herself
   On her lips.

And once she went to break a bough
   Of black alder.
15 She strayed so far she scarcely heard
   When he called her—

And didn't answer—didn't speak—
   Or return.
She stood, and then she ran and hid
20   In the fern.

He never found her, though he looked
   Everywhere,

And he asked at her mother's house
　　Was she there.

25 Sudden and swift and light as that
　　The ties gave,
And he learned of finalities
　　Besides the grave.

The Bonfire

"Oh, let's go up the hill and scare ourselves,
As reckless as the best of them to-night,
By setting fire to all the brush we piled
With pitchy hands to wait for rain or snow.
5 Oh, let's not wait for rain to make it safe.
The pile is ours: we dragged it bough on bough
Down dark converging paths between the pines.
Let's not care what we do with it to-night.
Divide it? No! But burn it as one pile
10 The way we piled it. And let's be the talk
Of people brought to windows by a light
Thrown from somewhere against their wall-paper.
Rouse them all, both the free and not so free
With saying what they'd like to do to us
15 For what they'd better wait till we have done.
Let's all but bring to life this old volcano,
If that is what the mountain ever was—
And scare ourselves. Let wild fire loose we will. . . ."

"And scare you too?" the children said together.

20 "Why wouldn't it scare me to have a fire
Begin in smudge with ropy smoke and know
That still, if I repent, I may recall it,
But in a moment not: a little spurt
Of burning fatness, and then nothing but
25 The fire itself can put it out, and that
By burning out, and before it burns out

It will have roared first and mixed sparks with stars,
And sweeping round it with a flaming sword,
Made the dim trees stand back in wider circle—
30   Done so much and I know not how much more
I mean it shall not do if I can bind it.
Well if it doesn't with its draft bring on
A wind to blow in earnest from some quarter,
As once it did with me upon an April.
35   The breezes were so spent with winter blowing
They seemed to fail the bluebirds under them
Short of the perch their languid flight was toward;
And my flame made a pinnacle to heaven
As I walked once round it in possession.
40   But the wind out of doors—you know the saying.
There came a gust. You used to think the trees
Made wind by fanning since you never knew
It blow but that you saw the trees in motion.
Something or someone watching made that gust.
45   It put the flame tip-down and dabbed the grass
Of over-winter with the least tip-touch
Your tongue gives salt or sugar in your hand.
The place it reached to blackened instantly.
The black was all there was by day-light,
50   That and the merest curl of cigarette smoke—
And a flame slender as the hepaticas,
Blood-root, and violets so soon to be now.
But the black spread like black death on the ground,
And I think the sky darkened with a cloud
55   Like winter and evening coming on together.
There were enough things to be thought of then.
Where the field stretches toward the north
And setting sun to Hyla brook, I gave it
To flames without twice thinking, where it verges

60   Upon the road, to flames too, though in fear
       They might find fuel there, in withered brake,
       Grass its full length, old silver golden-rod,
       And alder and grape vine entanglement,
       To leap the dusty deadline. For my own
65   I took what front there was beside. I knelt
       And thrust hands in and held my face away.
       Fight such a fire by rubbing not by beating.
       A board is the best weapon if you have it.
       I had my coat. And oh, I knew, I knew,
70   And said out loud, I couldn't bide the smother
       And heat so close in; but the thought of all
       The woods and town on fire by me, and all
       The town turned out to fight for me—that held me.
       I trusted the brook barrier, but feared
75   The road would fail; and on that side the fire
       Died not without a noise of crackling wood—
       Of something more than tinder-grass and weed—
       That brought me to my feet to hold it back
       By leaning back myself, as if the reins
80   Were round my neck and I was at the plough.
       I won! But I'm sure no one ever spread
       Another color over a tenth the space
       That I spread coal-black over in the time
       It took me. Neighbors coming home from town
85   Couldn't believe that so much black had come there
       While they had backs turned, that it hadn't been there
       When they had passed an hour or so before
       Going the other way and they not seen it.
       They looked about for someone to have done it.
90   But there was no one. I was somewhere wondering
       Where all my weariness had gone and why
       I walked so light on air in heavy shoes

In spite of a scorched Fourth-of-July feeling.
Why wouldn't I be scared remembering that?"

95   "If it scares you, what will it do to us?"

"Scare you. But if you shrink from being scared,
What would you say to war if it should come?
That's what for reasons I should like to know—
If you can comfort me by any answer."

100   "Oh, but war's not for children—it's for men."

"Now we are digging almost down to China.
My dears, my dears, you thought that—we all thought it.
So your mistake was ours. Haven't you heard, though,
About the ships where war has found them out
105   At sea, about the towns where war has come
Through opening clouds at night with droning speed
Further o'erhead than all but stars and angels,—
And children in the ships and in the towns?
Haven't you heard what we have lived to learn?
110   Nothing so new—something we had forgotten:
War is for everyone, for children too.
I wasn't going to tell you and I mustn't.
The best way is to come up hill with me
And have our fire and laugh and be afraid."

The Exposed Nest

You were forever finding some new play.
So when I saw you down on hands and knees
In the meadow, busy with the new-cut hay,
Trying, I thought, to set it up on end,
5   I went to show you how to make it stay,
If that was your idea, against the breeze,
And, if you asked me, even help pretend
To make it root again and grow afresh.
But 'twas no make-believe with you to-day,
10   Nor was the grass itself your real concern,
Though I found your hand full of wilted fern,
Steel-bright June-grass, and blackening heads of clover.
'Twas a nest full of young birds on the ground
The cutter-bar had just gone champing over
15   (Miraculously without tasting flesh)
And left defenseless to the heat and light.
You wanted to restore them to their right
Of something interposed between their sight
And too much world at once—could means be found.
20   The way the nest-full every time we stirred
Stood up to us as to a mother-bird
Whose coming home has been too long deferred,
Made me ask would the mother-bird return
And care for them in such a change of scene
25   And might our meddling make her more afraid.
That was a thing we could not wait to learn.
We saw the risk we took in doing good,
But dared not spare to do the best we could

Though harm should come of it; so built the screen
30 You had begun, and gave them back their shade.
All this to prove we cared. Why is there then
No more to tell? We turned to other things.
I haven't any memory—have you?—
Of ever coming to the place again
35 To see if the birds lived the first night through,
And so at last to learn to use their wings.

"Out, Out—"

The buzz-saw snarled and rattled in the yard
And made dust and dropped stove-length sticks of wood,
Sweet-scented stuff when the breeze drew across it.
And from there those that lifted eyes could count
5   Five mountain ranges one behind the other
Under the sunset far into Vermont.
And the saw snarled and rattled, snarled and rattled,
As it ran light, or had to bear a load.
And nothing happened: day was all but done.
10   Call it a day, I wish they might have said
To please the boy by giving him the half hour
That a boy counts so much when saved from work.
His sister stood beside them in her apron
To tell them "Supper." At the word, the saw,
15   As if to prove saws knew what supper meant,
Leaped out at the boy's hand, or seemed to leap—
He must have given the hand. However it was,
Neither refused the meeting. But the hand!
The boy's first outcry was a rueful laugh,
20   As he swung toward them holding up the hand
Half in appeal, but half as if to keep
The life from spilling. Then the boy saw all—
Since he was old enough to know, big boy
Doing a man's work, though a child at heart—
25   He saw all spoiled. "Don't let him cut my hand off—
The doctor, when he comes. Don't let him, sister!"
So. But the hand was gone already.
The doctor put him in the dark of ether.

He lay and puffed his lips out with his breath.
30   And then—the watcher at his pulse took fright.
No one believed. They listened at his heart.
Little—less—nothing!—and that ended it.
No more to build on there. And they, since they
Were not the one dead, turned to their affairs.

The Line-Gang

Here come the line-gang pioneering by.
They throw a forest down less cut than broken.
They plant dead trees for living, and the dead
They string together with a living thread.
5 They string an instrument against the sky
Wherein words whether beaten out or spoken
Will run as hushed as when they were a thought.
But in no hush they string it: they go past
With shouts afar to pull the cable taut,
10 To hold it hard until they make it fast,
To ease away—they have it. With a laugh,
An oath of towns that set the wild at naught
They bring the telephone and telegraph.

The Vanishing Red

He is said to have been the last Red Man
In Acton. And the Miller is said to have laughed—
If you like to call such a sound a laugh.
But he gave no one else a laugher's license.
5 For he turned suddenly grave as if to say,
"Whose business,—if I take it on myself,
Whose business—but why talk round the barn?—
When it's just that I hold with getting a thing done with."
You can't get back and see it as he saw it.
10 It's too long a story to go into now.
You'd have to have been there and lived it.
Then you wouldn't have looked on it as just a matter
Of who began it between the two races.

Some guttural exclamation of surprise
15 The Red Man gave in poking about the mill
Over the great big thumping shuffling mill-stone
Disgusted the Miller physically as coming
From one who had no right to be heard from.
"Come, John," he said, "you want to see the wheel pit?"

20 He took him down below a cramping rafter,
And showed him, through a manhole in the floor,
The water in desperate straits like frantic fish,
Salmon and sturgeon, lashing with their tails.
Then he shut down the trap door with a ring in it

25   That jangled even above the general noise,
     And came up stairs alone—and gave that laugh,
     And said something to a man with a meal-sack
     That the man with the meal-sack didn't catch—then.
     Oh, yes, he showed John the wheel pit all right.

The Sound of the Trees

I wonder about the trees.
Why do we wish to bear
Forever the noise of these
More than another noise
5 *So close to our dwelling place?*
We suffer them by the day
Till we lose all measure of pace,
And fixity in our joys,
And acquire a listening air.
10 *They are that that talks of going*
But never gets away;
And that talks no less for knowing,
As it grows wiser and older,
That now it means to stay.
15 *My feet tug at the floor*
And my head sways to my shoulder
Sometimes when I watch trees sway,
From the window or the door.
I shall set forth for somewhere,
20 *I shall make the reckless choice*
Some day when they are in voice
And tossing so as to scare
The white clouds over them on.
I shall have less to say,
25 *But I shall be gone.*